Manhattan Review®

Test Prep & Admissions Consulting

Turbocharge your GMAT: Integrated Reasoning Guide

part of the 6th Edition Series

- ☐ *Complete & challenging training sets*

- ☐ *Over 50 representative IR practice questions*

- ☐ *Great mix of Quant-based, Verbal-ba CR-based, and Logic-based IR questions*

- ☐ *Strategy to secure a perfect 8 score*

- ☐ *Enlisting process of solving each question type: TA, GI, Two-Part, and MSR*

- ☐ *Text-cum-graphic explanations: Multiple column-wise sorted images of tables*

- ☐ *Emphasis on logical deduction approach*

- ☐ *Computer-enabled IR formats: Table Analysis and Multi-Source Reasoning dealt with no compromise*

www.manhattanreview.com

Copyright and Terms of Use

Copyright and Trademark

All materials herein (including names, terms, trademarks, designs, images, and graphics) are the property of Manhattan Review, except where otherwise noted. Except as permitted herein, no such material may be copied, reproduced, displayed or transmitted or otherwise used without the prior written permission of Manhattan Review. You are permitted to use material herein for your personal, noncommercial use, provided that you do not combine such material into a combination, collection, or compilation of material. If you have any questions regarding the use of the material, please contact Manhattan Review at info@manhattanreview.com.

This material may make reference to countries and persons. The use of such references is for hypothetical and demonstrative purposes only.

Terms of Use

By using this material, you acknowledge and agree to the terms of use contained herein.

No Warranties

This material is provided without warranty, either express or implied, including the implied warranties of merchantability, of fitness for a particular purpose and noninfringement. Manhattan Review does not warrant or make any representations regarding the use, accuracy or results of the use of this material. This material may make reference to other source materials. Manhattan Review is not responsible in any respect for the content of such other source materials, and disclaims all warranties and liabilities with respect to the other source materials.

Limitation on Liability

Manhattan Review shall not be responsible under any circumstances for any direct, indirect, special, punitive, or consequential damages ("Damages") that may arise from the use of this material. In addition, Manhattan Review does not guarantee the accuracy or completeness of its course materials, which are provided "as is" with no warranty, express or implied. Manhattan Review assumes no liability for any Damages from errors or omissions in the material, whether arising in contract, tort or otherwise.

GMAT is a registered trademark of the Graduate Management Admission Council.
GMAC does not endorse, nor is it affiliated in any way with, the owner of this product or any content herein.

10-Digit International Standard Book Number: (ISBN: 1-62926-070-3)
13-Digit International Standard Book Number: (ISBN: 978-1-62926-070-9)

Last updated on April 20th, 2016.

Manhattan Review, 275 Madison Avenue, Suite 1429, New York, NY 10016.
Phone: +1 (212) 316-2000. E-Mail: info@manhattanreview.com. Web: www.manhattanreview.com

About the Turbocharge your GMAT Series

The Turbocharge Your GMAT Series is carefully designed to be clear, comprehensive, and content-driven. Long regarded as the gold standard in GMAT prep worldwide, Manhattan Review's GMAT prep books offer professional GMAT instruction for dramatic score improvement. Now in its updated 6th edition, the full series is designed to provide GMAT test-takers with complete guidance for highly successful outcomes. As many students have discovered, Manhattan Review's GMAT books break down the different test sections in a coherent, concise, and accessible manner. We delve deeply into the content of every single testing area and zero in on exactly what you need to know to raise your score. The full series is comprised of 16 guides that cover concepts in mathematics and grammar from the most basic through the most advanced levels, making them a great study resource for all stages of GMAT preparation. Students who work through all of our books benefit from a substantial boost to their GMAT knowledge and develop a thorough and strategic approach to taking the GMAT.

- ☐ GMAT Math Essentials (ISBN: 978-1-62926-057-0)
- ☐ GMAT Number Properties Guide (ISBN: 978-1-62926-058-7)
- ☐ GMAT Arithmetics Guide (ISBN: 978-1-62926-059-4)
- ☐ GMAT Algebra Guide (ISBN: 978-1-62926-060-0)
- ☐ GMAT Geometry Guide (ISBN: 978-1-62926-061-7)
- ☐ GMAT Word Problems Guide (ISBN: 978-1-62926-062-4)
- ☐ GMAT Sets & Statistics Guide (ISBN: 978-1-62926-063-1)
- ☐ GMAT Combinatorics & Probability Guide (ISBN: 978-1-62926-064-8)
- ☐ GMAT Data Sufficiency Guide (ISBN: 978-1-62926-065-5)
- ☐ GMAT Quantitative Question Bank (ISBN: 978-1-62926-066-2)
- ☐ GMAT Sentence Correction Guide (ISBN: 978-1-62926-067-9)
- ☐ GMAT Critical Reasoning Guide (ISBN: 978-1-62926-068-6)
- ☐ GMAT Reading Comprehension Guide (ISBN: 978-1-62926-069-3)
- ■ GMAT Integrated Reasoning Guide (ISBN: 978-1-62926-070-9)
- ☐ GMAT Analytical Writing Guide (ISBN: 978-1-62926-071-6)
- ☐ GMAT Vocabulary Builder (ISBN: 978-1-62926-072-3)

About the Company

Manhattan Review's origin can be traced directly back to an Ivy League MBA classroom in 1999. While teaching advanced quantitative subjects to MBAs at Columbia Business School in New York City, Professor Dr. Joern Meissner developed a reputation for explaining complicated concepts in an understandable way. Remembering their own less-than-optimal experiences preparing for the GMAT, Prof. Meissner's students challenged him to assist their friends, who were frustrated with conventional GMAT preparation options. In response, Prof. Meissner created original lectures that focused on presenting GMAT content in a simplified and intelligible manner, a method vastly different from the voluminous memorization and so-called tricks commonly offered by others. The new approach immediately proved highly popular with GMAT students, inspiring the birth of Manhattan Review.

Since its founding, Manhattan Review has grown into a multi-national educational services firm, focusing on GMAT preparation, MBA admissions consulting, and application advisory services, with thousands of highly satisfied students all over the world. The original lectures have been continuously expanded and updated by the Manhattan Review team, an enthusiastic group of master GMAT professionals and senior academics. Our team ensures that Manhattan Review offers the most time-efficient and cost-effective preparation available for the GMAT. Please visit www.ManhattanReview.com for further details.

About the Founder

Professor Dr. Joern Meissner has more than 25 years of teaching experience at the graduate and undergraduate levels. He is the founder of Manhattan Review, a worldwide leader in test prep services, and he created the original lectures for its first GMAT preparation class. Prof. Meissner is a graduate of Columbia Business School in New York City, where he received a PhD in Management Science. He has since served on the faculties of prestigious business schools in the United Kingdom and Germany. He is a recognized authority in the areas of supply chain management, logistics, and pricing strategy. Prof. Meissner thoroughly enjoys his research, but he believes that grasping an idea is only half of the fun. Conveying knowledge to others is even more fulfilling. This philosophy was crucial to the establishment of Manhattan Review, and remains its most cherished principle.

The Advantages of Using Manhattan Review

▶ **Time efficiency and cost effectiveness.**

– For most people, the most limiting factor of test preparation is time.

– It takes significantly more teaching experience to prepare a student in less time.

– Our test preparation approach is tailored for busy professionals. We will teach you what you need to know in the least amount of time.

▶ **Our high-quality and dedicated instructors are committed to helping every student reach her/his goals.**

International Phone Numbers and Official Manhattan Review Websites

Manhattan Headquarters	+1-212-316-2000	www.manhattanreview.com
USA & Canada	+1-800-246-4600	www.manhattanreview.com
Argentina	+1-212-316-2000	www.review.com.ar
Australia	+61-3-9001-6618	www.manhattanreview.com
Austria	+43-720-115-549	www.review.at
Belgium	+32-2-808-5163	www.manhattanreview.be
Brazil	+1-212-316-2000	www.manhattanreview.com.br
Chile	+1-212-316-2000	www.manhattanreview.cl
China	+86-20-2910-1913	www.manhattanreview.cn
Czech Republic	+1-212-316-2000	www.review.cz
France	+33-1-8488-4204	www.review.fr
Germany	+49-89-3803-8856	www.review.de
Greece	+1-212-316-2000	www.review.com.gr
Hong Kong	+852-5808-2704	www.review.hk
Hungary	+1-212-316-2000	www.review.co.hu
India	+1-212-316-2000	www.review.in
Indonesia	+1-212-316-2000	www.manhattanreview.id
Ireland	+1-212-316-2000	www.gmat.ie
Italy	+39-06-9338-7617	www.manhattanreview.it
Japan	+81-3-4589-5125	www.manhattanreview.jp
Malaysia	+1-212-316-2000	www.review.my
Mexico	+1-212-316-2000	www.manhattanreview.mx
Netherlands	+31-20-808-4399	www.manhattanreview.nl
New Zealand	+1-212-316-2000	www.review.co.nz
Philippines	+1-212-316-2000	www.review.ph
Poland	+1-212-316-2000	www.review.pl
Portugal	+1-212-316-2000	www.review.pt
Qatar	+1-212-316-2000	www.review.qa
Russia	+1-212-316-2000	www.manhattanreview.ru
Singapore	+65-3158-2571	www.gmat.sg
South Africa	+1-212-316-2000	www.manhattanreview.co.za
South Korea	+1-212-316-2000	www.manhattanreview.kr
Sweden	+1-212-316-2000	www.gmat.se
Spain	+34-911-876-504	www.review.es
Switzerland	+41-435-080-991	www.review.ch
Taiwan	+1-212-316-2000	www.gmat.tw
Thailand	+66-6-0003-5529	www.manhattanreview.com
Turkey	+1-212-316-2000	www.review.com.tr
United Arab Emirates	+1-212-316-2000	www.manhattanreview.ae
United Kingdom	+44-20-7060-9800	www.manhattanreview.co.uk
Rest of World	+1-212-316-2000	www.manhattanreview.com

Contents

Chapter 1

Introduction

Dear Students,

Here at Manhattan Review, we constantly strive to provide you the best educational content for standardized test preparation. We make a tremendous effort to keep making things better and better for you. This is especially important with respect to an examination such as the GMAT: the typical GMAT aspirant is confused with so many test-prep options available. Your challenge is to choose a book or a tutor that prepares you for attaining your goal. We cannot not say that we are one of the best. It is you who has to be the judge of that.

The greatest challenge to any test-prep companies is how to present interactive contents in text form. It was challenge for us, too. We hope you have seen IR books by other leading test-prep companies; if not, please do look at them. While they have done a fairly good job presenting content online, they have failed miserably at producing traditional textbooks.

Why did they fail?

Since the Table Analysis and Multi-Source Reasoning IR questions are interactive prompts in the test, it is a challenge—even for the leading test-prep companies—to effectively present and explain the content. The ones who dared come up with IR books have only provided a few questions with no, or few, practice questions. Their textbooks are mere supplementary material to their online content.

We are proud that we have met the challenge of presenting interactive prompts. This book is a landmark, in that it presents computer-enabled, interactive content, enriched with never-before-seen graphics.

The Manhattan Review's Integrated Reasoning book is holistic and comprehensive in all respects. Should you have any queries, please feel free to write to me at *info@manhattanreview.com*.

Happy Learning!

Prof. Dr. Joern Meissner
& The Manhattan Review Team

Chapter 2

What is Integrated Reasoning?

2.1 Integrated Reasoning in the GMAT

Over the years, the GMAT test has been an undisputed measure of test takers' ability to show-case the skills that matter most in the business-school classroom.

However, did the old GMAT tests still miss something?

It was great at predicting academic success in B-school; however, B-school teaching methodology involves applying case studies. The old GMAT tested your quantitative and verbal ability, but real-world data are not restricted to only quantitative and verbal data. In fact, complex information can be presented in the form of a graph, text with quantitative information, data in a tabular format, and text with verbal information. In a nutshell, to make a meaningful business decision, one may need to integrate multiple types of information.

Critical Reasoning prompts test verbal reasoning, but seldom quantitative reasoning; its scope is narrow. Integrated Reasoning prompts on the other hand, are more comprehensive.

2.2 What does Integrated Reasoning measure?

GMAC states that the Integrated Reasoning section measures your ability to comprehend and evaluate multiple types of information: textual, tabular, graphic, visual, quantitative, and verbal, that it applies quantitative and verbal reasoning to solve problems in relation to one another. This section differs from the Quantitative and Verbal sections in two ways:

(1) IR comprises both quantitative and verbal reasoning, and

(2) IR prompts use four different response formats rather than only the traditional multiple-choice format used for Quantitative and Verbal questions.

The four types of questions used in the Integrated Reasoning section are:

(1) Table analysis

(2) Graphics interpretation

(3) Two-part analysis

(4) Multi-source reasoning

In a nutshell, the IR questions assess your ability to apply, infer, evaluate, recognize, and strategize information from multiple sources.

2.3 Types of IR Questions

Apply Questions

Apply questions measure your ability to comprehend the concepts in the information given and apply them to a new situation.

Evaluate and Inference Questions

Evaluate questions measure your ability to make decisions based on the quality of information. These questions are very similar to Critical Reasoning questions, in which you are asked if the information strengthens/weakens the argument, if there is sufficient information to make a decision (some aspect of data sufficiency), plus inference and flaws in reasoning.

Recognize Questions

Recognize questions measure your ability to identify in the information some facts or aspects and their relationships. You may be asked to recognize agreement and disagreement, strength of correlation between two variables, compare two or more data points, or understand data and deduce information.

Strategize Questions

Strategize questions test your ability to gain an objective within the constraints. You may be asked to select a course of action that gives desired results, while optimizing resources.

2.4 What are the Different Parts of Integrated Reasoning?

As stated earlier that there are four parts to Integrated Reasoning: Table Analysis, Graphics Interpretation, Two-Part Analysis, Multi-Source Reasoning.

Let us look at them one by one.

2.4.1 Table Analysis

The Table Analysis questions present a table similar to a spreadsheet. The table can be sorted only in ascending order on any of its columns, by selecting the column's title from a drop-down menu given above the table. A brief text explaining the table is usually provided. The question presents three statements, values, or expressions. You may be asked whether each statement is true or false, or if "Yes" or "No" can be inferred from the information.

You may be asked to calculate mean, median, or range, calculate ratios, proportions, or probabilities, recognize correlations between two sets of data, compare a data in relation to other data, or select a statement that best helps explain the data given in prompt.

As with MSR datasets, Table Analysis prompts are interactive.

A sample TA Question

The table presents the Average Maximum Score, Average Minimum Score, and the Intelligence Quotient for grade X and XII students of City International School for six months.

Months ▼

Months	Grade	Average maximum Score	Average minimum Score	Intelligence Quotient	
July	X	71	55	115	16
July	XII	72	45	116	
August	X	66 *67*	58	116	8
August	XII	68	55	120	
September	X	72	52	121	20
September	XII	75	56	114	19
October	X	68	54	121	14
October	XII	69	45	120	24
November	X	81	62	119	17
November	XII	69	51	118	18
December	X	71	52	117	19
December	XII	70	49	114	21

For each of the following statements, select "Yes" if the statement is true based on the information provided; otherwise, select "No."

	Yes	No	
A	○	○	Compared to grade XII students, grade X students are more consistent with regards to the Intelligence Quotients attribute, taking range as a parameter to measure the consistency.
B	○	○	For any of the given months, the greatest deviation of the Average Maximum Score and Average Minimum Score for grade XII students is more than that for grade X students.
C	○	○	The mean average minimum score for August is more than that for July and for December.

2.4.2 Graphics Interpretation

Graphics Interpretation questions present a chart, graph, diagram, or other visual form of information. The chart is followed by two fill-In-the-blank type statements. You have to "fill in the blank" by choosing the best option from a drop-down menu.

Graphics Interpretation questions include column charts, line graphs, pie charts, Venn diagrams, scatterplots, bubble graphs, flow charts, organization charts, and strategy maps.

Unlike Table Analysis and MSR prompts, Graphic Analysis prompts are static.

A Sample GI Question

The bar graph shows the number of unemployed youth in a country for seven years.

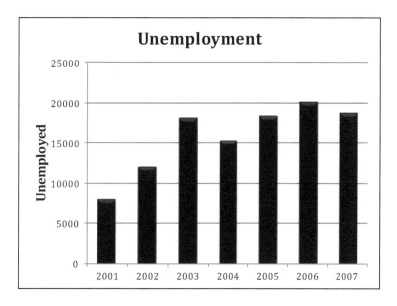

Based on the given information, use the drop-down menu to most accurately complete the following statements:

A. The greatest increase in the number of unemployed youth from any year to the succeeding year is approximately

3736
4452
6108
7542

B. The number of unemployed youth in the year 2004 is approximately percent of the number of unemployed youth in the year 2003.

16
19.5
84
119.5

Other Types of GI Charts/Diagrams

Multiple Column Chart

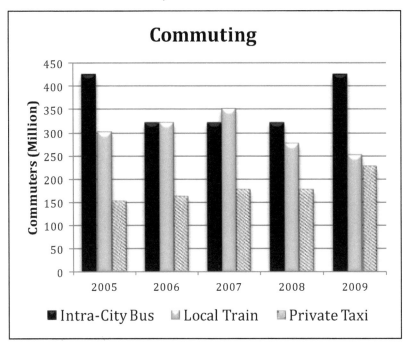

Pie chart

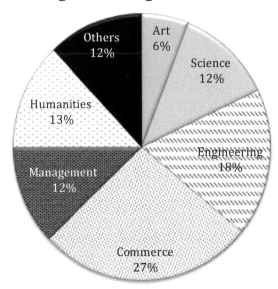

Bubble chart

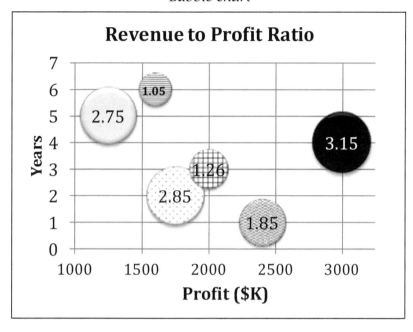

Scatter Plot

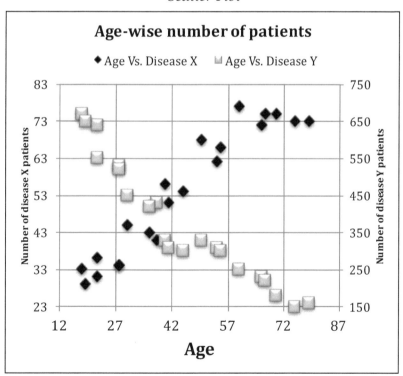

Strategy Map

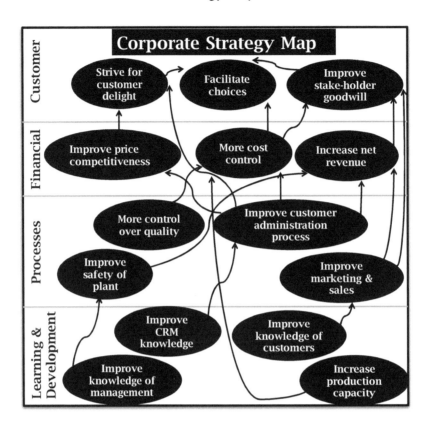

2.4.3 Two-Part Analysis

Two-Part Analysis questions present a small passage or quantitative problem. There are two correct choices related to the information given. The choices are given in a tabular format. The possible answers are listed in the third column. You have to select one choice in each column. The question may test you on GMAT mathematical concepts, say, two aspects of a right-circular cylinder—Height and Diameter. Similarly, for verbal concepts, it may ask questions on strengthening/weakening the argument, inferable/not inferable premises, assumption/fact distinction, existence of cause/effect, characteristics/predictions distinctions, or strategies applicable for, say, companies X and Y.

Unlike the Table Analysis and MSR prompts, but like Graphics Interpretation prompts, Two-Part Analysis prompts are static.

Sample Two-Part Questions

A Quant-Based Two-Part Question:

For a right circular cylinder, r stands for the radius of its base, h for its height, A for its curved surface area, and V for its volume. In terms of the variables A and V, select in the table the expressions that represent height h and radius r.

Make only two selections, one in each column.

	A	B	
	r	h	
A	○	○	$\frac{A^2}{4\pi V}$
B	○	○	$\frac{2V}{A}$
C	○	○	$\frac{A^2 V}{8\pi}$
D	○	○	$\frac{2A}{V}$
E	○	○	$\frac{A}{V}$

A Verbal-Based Two-Part Question:

Consultant: "The decline in market share of the Whito 3-kg detergent pack is a matter of concern. There could be many predictive reasons. The competing brand, EcoWash, is always on the lookout to gain Whito's substantial market share. Also, due to adverse judgments in consumer courts against WhiteMagic detergent—the brand that kept EcoWash's detergent sales in check—WhiteMagic's sales are suffering, providing an opportunity for EcoWash. Usually, customers prefer the detergent from the brand that already has an established soap cake selling in the market."

Indicate in the table which cause-and-effect sequence would most likely, according to the consultant, result in a decline of market share of Whito detergent.

Make two selections, one in each column.

	A	B	
	Cause	Effect	
A	○	○	An increase in the market share of EcoWash soap cake
B	○	○	An increase in the market share of EcoWash detergent
C	○	○	An increase in the market share of WhiteMagic detergent
D	○	○	A decrease in the market share of EcoWash soap cake
E	○	○	A decrease in the market share of EcoWash detergent

2.4.4   Multi-Source Reasoning

As the name suggests, Multi-Source reasoning questions comprise information from more than one source. An MSR question will have two or three tabs of information; however, you can view only one tab at a time, by clicking it. The tab may contain a written passages, graphs, diagrams, tables, or/and other types of visual information.

A typical MSR dataset will have three questions; however, you will find three to six questions in *Official Guide* per dataset. There are two question formats for Multi-Source Reasoning:

(1) Multiple-choice questions

(2) Multiple-dichotomous choice questions

For multiple-choice questions, five answer choices given. You have to select the correct answer choice. Multiple-dichotomous question presents three statements, values, or expressions. You may be asked whether, according to the information, each statement is True/False, Agreeable/Not Agreeable, Acceptable/Not Acceptable, Supported/Not Supported, or can be inferable/Not inferable. As with Table Analysis prompts, MSR prompts are interactive.

A sample MSR Question

Tab 1

Mike, Chief economist, on BRICS countries	Professor Walter on BRICS countries

The notion that the era of emerging BRICS countries is over—and that among them only China would make it to the group of high-income countries—is outlandish. No doubt the growth rates in the BRICS group of Brazil, Russia, India, China, and South Africa have been affected by the global slowdown, and countries such as India have been further singed by capital-flow reversals. However, this is a temporary phenomenon that will peter out sooner rather than later. The BRICS countries' economies are bound to reinvent the global economic order—and even fashion it in their own image—once the macroeconomic balances are restored and foreign investment flows rebound, boosted by reforms.

Similarly, the argument that the rest of the BRICS countries will fall by the wayside while China continues to march ahead is flawed. China's growth rate is almost half that of peak levels. It's also facing a double whammy: 1) its export-led economy has been badly hit by the slowdown in advanced country markets, and 2) rising wages and a shortage of skills erode its competitive base, as it struggles to shift over to a domestic consumption-based growth model. This will probably help other BRICS countries, such as India, make new inroads into the global markets for manufactured goods, and thus close in fast on China.

In fact, the most recent trends on the global Greenfield investments, which exclude mergers and acquisitions, validate this argument. The numbers show that while the new FDI (Foreign Direct Investment) projects in China have almost halved after the global slowdown, the other BRICS countries haven't been so badly bruised. On the contrary, the gap between China and other BRICS countries has in fact shrunk, with India accounting for 30% of the Greenfield FDI projects, as compared to China's 40% share.

Tab 2

| Mike, Chief economist, on BRICS countries | Professor Walter on BRICS countries |

The economist's assessment that the BRICS era is at an end is right on the money. Despite witnessing robust economic growth in the last decade, each of the BRICS countries faces a unique set of problems today. The recent global economic downturn has exposed structural infirmities that will prevent these economies from returning to a high-growth trajectory anytime soon. Besides, it is not realistic to expect these emerging markets to grow faster from a higher GDP base rather than from their previous low threshold.

In India, the economy is wracked by a Rupee in free-fall, high inflation, and a burgeoning current account deficit. Recent months have seen significant capital outflows, with foreign investors opting to park their funds in a recovering U.S. economy. The petering-out of growth sentiments is directly related to the political leadership's failure to affect a much-needed second wave of economic reforms. Furthermore, with policy paralysis expected to continue, the India-growth story remains in limbo. In both Brazil and Russia, the weakening of commodity prices has hit the economies hard, exposing their over-reliance on natural resources as cash cows. Meanwhile, South Africa's economy has been hurting since a recession that affected several crucial industries. In China, the economy is transitioning from resource-intensive, investment-led growth to a consumption-oriented pattern. Add to this the massive global pressure to appreciate the Yuan, and it is clear that China would need to affect a not-so-easy overhaul of its economic model to maintain high growth. However, as the economist points out, given China's planned economic model and ability to move resources without political missteps, it is best placed from among the BRICS nations to pull out of the middle-income trap. Taken together, the global heft that the BRICS bloc wielded is over. While these emerging markets will continue to grow, they will need to get used to moderate rates of growth.

Question:

For each of the following issues, select "Agree" if, based on the information provided, it can be inferred that both the commentators would hold similar positions on the issue. Otherwise, select "Disagree."

	Agree	Disagree	
A	○	○	Acknowledging that the BRICS countries had experienced good economic growth in the past
B	○	○	The timeframe in which the BRICS countries will bounce back to good economic growth
C	○	○	China's ability to transform into a consumption-oriented economy soon

Number of questions in IR section

There are 12 prompts in the IR section. The following breakdown is a possible part-wise distribution:

- *Table Analysis:* 2–3 questions

- *Two-Parts:* 3–4 questions

- *Graphics Interpretation:* 2–4 questions

- *Multi-Source Reasoning:* 3 questions, 1 dataset

The Calculator

The new GMAT test window will provide you with a simple calculator at all times during the Integrated Reasoning section but not during other sections.

The calculator link is located at the upper-left corner of the test window.

Do Use the Calculator

IR quant-based problems may have messy numbers. You must attempt these questions within a limited time period, so when you face lengthy calculations or messy numbers, use the calculator.

2.5 How is the Integrated Reasoning Section Scored?

IR scores range from 1–8, with an increment of one point. Out of 12 prompts, there are a few experimental questions. How many experimental questions are there in an IR section is not yet known.

How to achieve a perfect 8?

The IR scoring algorithm is difficult to predict. However, the following table can guide you towards achieving a perfect score of 8:

Number of correct questions	IR Score
9–12	8
8–9	7
7–8	6
6–7	5
5–6	4
4–5	3
2–3	2
0–1	1

This table is only hypothetical. The scoring will depend on the number of experimental questions, and also on the difficulty level of the questions you answered correctly; however remember that the IR section is not an adaptive test. To be safe, assume that to get a score of 8, you must answer at least 9–10 questions correctly.

How to get 9–10 questions correct?

Attempting not-so-familiar IR types of questions may eat up your time. Twelve prompts in 30 minutes means you get 2.5 minutes per prompt. You very well may be short of time in the IR section. Note also that there are 1–3 parts (subquestions) per prompt. Every part has to be correct for you to get the credit for the prompt. There is no partial credit.

Only the Two-Part questions are similar to Quantitative and Verbal ones. So, you should try to do each Two-Part question in less than 2.5 minutes.

You should attempt all Graphics Interpretation questions, as they only have two parts (subquestions), whereas the Table Analysis and some Multi-Source Reasoning questions have three parts (subquestions).

Though some of the long tables in Table Analysis questions may seem scary, but don't go by the size of the tables. You have to focus on a particular parts of the tables. So, do attempt all the TA questions.

Multi-Source Reasoning questions are the most unfamiliar and time-consuming. There may be 2-3 tabs of information, with three prompts per dataset. So, if your exam clock shows only 2.5

minutes left and you get an MSR dataset, you may not be able to attempt even one prompt—as reading 2–3 wordy tabs of information may take more than three minutes.

The following strategy table below may guide you:

Question Type	Number of parts per question	Average time per part	Recommendation
Two-Part	2	2.5/2 = 1.25′	Should attempt
Graphic Interpretation	2	2.5/2 = 1.25′	Should attempt
Table Analysis	3	2.5/3 = 0.83′	Although the average time per part is less than one minute, you really should attempt the TA questions, because most of them are quant-based and thus less wordy compared to the MSR-dataset ones.
Multi-Source Reasoning (3 prompts/ dataset)	1 for Multiple Choice questions 3 for Dichotomous Choice questions	1.1′–1.5′	If you are hard-pressed for time, guess on MSR prompts. The major drawback of this type is that, as with the RC type, the MSR dataset has at least three questions and 2–3 tabs of information. The first question invariably takes 4–5 minutes.

Chapter 3

Table Analysis

3.1 Strategies and Concepts

As stated earlier, Table Analysis questions have you use an interactive table similar to a spread sheet, so you must get experience working with Microsoft Excel tables. Table Analysis data are real-life data and thus may sometimes look ugly. You can infer Information from them using the listing property and sorting capability of these tables. However, in the GMAT-IR section, you can sort tables only in ascending order; you do not have the luxury of other Excel features, such as being able to calculate difference, ratio, mean, median, standard deviation, correlation factor, etc.

3.2 Commonly Tested Concepts in Table Analysis

Concepts commonly tested in Table Analysis (TA) are listed below. These include calculating the absolute difference between values, inferring through sorting, and finding mean, median, and mode. You will be asked to apply the concepts of measures of dispersion, and calculate absolute deviation, standard deviation, and range.

- *Calculate absolute deviation*

  A TA question may ask you to compare the difference of values given in two columns. For instance, it may ask you to mark "Yes" or "No" for the statement: *"Among the listed 22 cities, City X has the least deviation between Maximum Temperature per day and Minimum Temperature per day."*

- *Sort and infer*

  Sorting is a table feature you will use the most. You must utilize it to the fullest. A typical table may have 4–10 columns, and 7–25 rows.

  For instance, you may have to mark "Yes" or "No" for: *"All cities that have a Maximum Temperature per day more than* $39°F$ *have as their Minimum Temperature per day at least* $100°F$.*"* Your most efficient approach is to sort (by default, ascending order only) the cities by maximum temperature per day. You can quickly locate the cells with maximum

19

temperature more than 39°F, and then glance at the corresponding cells in the column of minimum temperature per day. If all the cells have values more than or equal to 39°F, you mark "Yes," else "No".

- *Mean, Median, and Mode*

  The concepts of median and mean are widely tested in TA prompts.

  » *Mean*

    Although there may be many types of mean, from the GMAT-IR's perspective, it is simple means and weighted means that are important.

    ◦ *Simple mean*

      Simple mean is nothing but the age-old concept: *"Sum of all numerical entities divided by the number of entities."* Compared to calculating the median, calculating the mean may be calculation-intensive. However, you need not always calculate its exact value in TA prompts. You can infer it by applying logical approaches. This book has a couple of great examples with the application of logical approaches.

    ◦ *Weighted mean*

      Weighted mean is indeed a mean, but as opposed to the simple mean, in which each entity has equal importance or weight, the weighted mean takes into account varying importance or weight of each entity.

      Let's take a question: *"If in a class of 40 boys and 60 girls, the percentage score of boys is 75%, and that of girls is 85%, what is the percentage score of the entire class?*

      The simple mean would be computed by adding the two percentages and dividing the sum by the number of entities (two) , i.e., $(75 + 85)/2 = 80\%$.

      However, the computed simple mean 80% is wrong. Since there are more girls than boys, the girls' percentage would have more weight in the total class percentage.

      Weighted mean =

      $$\frac{\left[(\text{Boys' \% score} \times \text{number of boys}) + (\text{Girls' \% score} \times \text{number of girls})\right]}{\text{Total number of students}}$$

      $$\Rightarrow \text{Weighted mean (score)} = \frac{\left[(75\% \times 40) + (85\% \times 60)\right]}{100} = \frac{(30\% + 51\%)}{100} = 81\%$$

» *Median*

Median is also a widely tested concept in TA prompts. Median is the middle-most value of a data set when the data are arranged in ascending order (or descending order, but you can sort tables only in ascending order). To find out the median, you have to sort the table by the appropriate column.

$$\text{Median} = \text{Value of } \left(\tfrac{n+1}{2}\right)^{\text{th}} \text{cell}, \qquad n = \text{number of rows}$$

If the number of rows is even, we take the simple mean of the values of two middle-most cells.

$$\text{Median} = \text{Mean of } \left[\left(\tfrac{n}{2}\right)^{\text{th}} \text{cell} + \left(\tfrac{n}{2} + 1\right)^{\text{th}} \text{cell}\right], \qquad n = \text{number of rows}$$

» *Mode*

Although the *Official Guide* writes about mode, it has not been tested so far.

- *Dispersion*

An easy-to-understand definition of "dispersion" is "Spread of data." For instance, for a series 10, 10, 12, 14, 16, 17, 17, and 20, the spread of data is from 10 to 20.

- *Deviation*

Deviation is a measure of how far data are from the average value. Each datapoint will have its value of deviation with respect to the average.

Say, for example, you have a series: 10, 12, 14, 16, 18, 20, 22, 24, 26, 28, and 30. The average (or, in this case, also the mean) of the series is 20. So, the deviations are:

Data point (X)	10	12	14	16	18	20	22	24	26	28	30
Deviation (X − 20)	−10	−8	−6	−4	−2	0	2	4	6	8	10

Note that the farther a data point is from the mean, the greater is the deviation.

- *Range*

Range is tested in TA questions. Range of a series is the difference of Highest & Lowest values of data points in a series.

Range of a series = Highest value − Lowest value

In the example above, Range = 30 − 10 = 20.

- *Standard Deviation*

Deviation yields the value of deviation for each data point. Range yields a single value of deviation for the whole series but takes into account only the highest and the lowest values; however Standard deviation takes each data point into consideration yet yields a single value of deviation for the whole series.

You need not know the mathematical formula to calculate standard deviation. An IR question will never ask you to calculate the value. Mere understanding of the concept is sufficient.

For those who are curious to know, this is the definition of Standard Deviation (SD):

> *Standard deviation (SD) is the positive square root of the mean of squared deviations.*

It may not be easy to comprehend the definition, but you need not understand how the SD is calculated. Here are three examples to help you better understand it:

Example 1 Data Points: 10   10   10   10   10   10   10   10   10   10
Mean = 10, Range = 0, SD = 0.

Example 2 Data Points: 10   10   10   10   10   20   20   20   20   20
Mean = 15, Range = 10, SD = 5.

Example 3 Data Points: 10   11   12   14   16   16   11   17   17   20
Mean = 15.1, Range = 10, SD = 3.08.

- *Correlation*

Correlation is a measure of relationships between any two entities. Two entities are positively correlated if both of them either increase in tandem or decrease in tandem, whereas the entities are negatively correlated if one entity decreases in value while the other entity increases in value, or vice versa. The entities are not correlated if the increase or decrease in the value of one entity cannot be concluded relative to the increase or decrease in the value of the other.

We will discuss this concept with the help of an example.

3.3 Process of Solving TA Questions

(1) *Understand the data set*

Read the question narration and the column headings of the table. Try to understand the relationship of a column with other column(s). Sometimes column headings are not very expressive; however, you can get information about them from the question narration or any note given outside the table area.

Don't be intimidated by the number of rows and number of columns. You will have to deal with only two to three columns and a few rows at a time. Quickly scan through the data given in the table. By doing this, you will grasp whether the data is given in integers or in some ugly numbers in decimal form. If the data is given in decimals, don't be intimidated. You can always approximate them to make manageable integers.

(2) *Understand the question*

As you know, that there are three dichotomous statement type questions in a TA dataset. You have to mark each statement with either "Yes" or "No". Remember that there is no partial credit for correct response(s); each of the three responses must be correct for you to get the credit for the question.

Read the question statement and understand it. Rephrase the statement in your words, and if needed, translate it into mathematical language.

(3) *Develop an approach*

There could be two or more ways to approach a question. You may figure out that a question requires two-way sorting, but you can sort the table by one column at a time. So, figure out the best approach to solve the question.

(4) *Apply the approach*

Apply your approach and click the correct radio button. You should jot down the results of any calculations you do. It is likely that you might need one or two results from previous questions as intermediate steps for answering the questions that follow.

3.4 Examples

Here are few GMAT-like questions.

In an actual GMAT exam, you will select columns to sort using a drop-down menu. In this book, we obviously cannot provide such menus. This does not mean that, as with the other renowned IR textbooks, that you cannot solve problems. We have provided you images of sorted tables for each question.

To practice questions on your own, write to us at *info@manhattanreview.com*, we will send you filter-enabled tables, so you can practice in a computer-enabled environment.

Example 1

The table shows area, population, and population density for 11 towns.

Town	Area ('000 square mile)	Population (Million)	Population Density ('000 people/sq. mile)
A	2.5	4.89	1.96
B	1.6	5.26	3.29
C	4.58	6.78	1.48
D	3.52	8.25	2.34
E	6.87	12.65	1.84
F	9.12	13.58	1.49
G	5.23	12.75	2.44
H	8	16.3	2.04
I	2.68	15.35	5.73
J	9	24.54	2.73
K	4.56	25.54	5.60

For each of the following statements, select "Yes" if the statement is true based on the information provided; otherwise, select "No".

	Yes	No	
A	○	○	Population density of town *D* represents the median population density of all the towns.
B	○	○	The town with the highest population density also has the highest population among all the towns.
C	○	○	The town with the lowest population density also has the smallest area among all the towns.

Solution, Part A

The question wants you to find out whether population density (P.D.) of town D = the median population density of all the towns.

To get the value of the median population density, sort the table by column 4 (Population Density):

Sorted by column 4

Col 1	Col 2	Col 3	Col 4
Town	**Area ('000 square miles)**	**Population (Million)**	**Population Density ('000 people/sq. miles)**
C	4.58	6.78	1.48
F	9.12	13.58	1.49
E	6.87	12.65	1.84
A	2.5	4.89	1.96
H	8	16.3	2.04
D	3.52	8.25	2.34
G	5.23	12.75	2.44
J	9	24.54	2.73
B	1.6	5.26	3.29
K	4.56	25.54	5.60
I	2.68	15.35	5.73

Median of P. D.

= Value of P. D. for $(\frac{11+1}{2})^{\text{th}}$ town

= Value of P. D. for 6th town

= 2.34

There are 11 rows/towns, thus the middle-most value (Median) in column 4 after sorting it would be the value of $\frac{11+1}{2}$ = 6th town = 2.34.

The population density of town D = median population density of all the towns = 2.34.

The answer for Part A is "Yes."

Solution, Part B

The question wants you to find out whether the town that has the highest population density is the same as the one that has the highest population.

Looking at the table, you find that town I has the highest population density = 5.73 units, but town K, not I, has the highest population = 25.54 Million among all the towns.

The answer for the part B is "No".

Solution, Part C

The question wants you to find out whether the town with the lowest population density is the same as the one that has the smallest area.

Looking again at the table, you find that town C has the lowest population density = 1.48 units, but town B has the smallest area = 1.6 units among all the towns.

The answer for the part C is "No".

Example 2

The table presents quarterly sales and inventory data, in metric tons (MT), for Apex Corporation for a few steel products.

S - Sales (MT); I - Inventory (MT)

Products	Quarter I		Quarter II		Quarter III		Quarter IV		Yearly Total	
	S	I	S	I	S	I	S	I	S	I
CR pipe	24	12	15	8	4	8	13	4	56	32
CR sheet	16	8	12	12	16	4	15	21	59	45
CR tube	15	15	16	8	6	15	8	4	45	42
CR wire	15	0	24	8	18	13	13	12	70	33
HR pipe	24	12	21	8	5	21	12	15	62	56
HR sheet	18	15	15	16	0	0	14	3	47	34
HR tube	8	9	8	21	8	0	9	2	33	32
HR wire	24	26	12	16	15	15	8	4	59	61
HS Billet	21	24	21	0	18	5	15	12	75	41
MS Billet	10	8	15	0	18	2	15	16	58	26
Total	175	129	159	97	108	83	122	93	564	402

For each of the following statements, select "Yes" if the statement is true based on the information provided; otherwise select "No".

	Yes	No	
A	○	○	In quarter II, among all products, CR tube sale is least deviated from the arithmetic mean sale for that quarter.
B	○	○	In quarter IV, among all the products, highest sales-to-inventory ratio was observed for HR tubes.
C	○	○	Median sale for quarter I is more than that for each of the other three quarters.

Solution, Part A

The question wants you to find out whether in the Q2, the deviation (difference) of CR tube sale from the Q2 arithmetic mean sale is less than that of other products.

In other way, the question statement states that for Q2, the sales of CR tube is closest to Q2 mean sales.

Mathematically, this means:

$$|\text{CR tube sales} - \text{mean sales for Q2}| < |\text{Other products' sales} - \text{mean sales for Q2}|.$$

First, you calculate the mean sales for Q2.

Since

$$\text{Total Q2 sales} = 159 \text{ MT,}$$

and

$$\text{Total number of products} = 10,$$

then

$$\text{Q2 mean sales} = 159/10 = 15.9 \text{ MT.}$$

So,

$$|\text{CR Tube sales} - \text{mean sales for Q2}| = |16 - 15.9| = 0.1.$$

Run through the values in column 4 (Q2 sales) and mentally deduct each value from 15.9. You will find that the deviation of CR Tube sales = 0.1 is the lowest among that of all the other products.

The answer for part A is "Yes."

Solution, Part B

The question wants you to find out whether in the Q4, the ratio of sales to inventory for HR tubes is more than that for other products.

Mathematically, this means that for Q4,

$$\left[\frac{\text{Sales}}{\text{Inventory}}\right]_{\text{HR tube}} > \left[\frac{\text{Sales}}{\text{Inventory}}\right]_{\text{Other products}}$$

$$\Rightarrow \quad \left[\frac{\text{Sales}}{\text{Inventory}}\right]_{\text{HR tube}} = 9/2 = 4.5.$$

You have nine products for which you need to calculate the sales-to-inventory ratio, but that would be too time-consuming, and hence it is not advisable to compute.

A better approach would be to calculate a few select values. You know that for HR tubes, the value is 4.5, which is more than 1. You can skip the products for which sales are less than their inventory as the sales-to-inventory ratio value would be less than 1. Secondly, you can mentally divide sales by inventory to get probable contenders that have values, equalling more than 4. There is only one such product: HR sheets, which has a sales-to-inventory value equal to $14/3 = 4.67$, more than 4.5, so the statement is wrong.

The answer for part B is "No".

Solution, Part C

The question wants you to find out whether median sales for Q1 is more than median sales for each of Q2, Q3, and Q4.

Mathematically, this means:

$$\text{Median sales}\big|_{Q1} > \text{Median sales}\big|_{\text{any other quarter}}$$

To get the median sales of each quarter, sort the table by its sales columns to get the table:

Sorted by Q1 Sales (Column 2)			Sorted by Q2 Sales (Column 4)			Sorted by Q3 Sales (Column 6)			Sorted by Q4 Sales (Column 8)		
Col 1	Col 2	Col 3	Col 1	Col 4	Col 5	Col 1	Col 6	Col 7	Col 1	Col 8	Col 9
Products	**Quarter I**		**Products**	**Quarter II**		**Products**	**Quarter III**		**Products**	**Quarter IV**	
	S	**I**		**S**	**I**		**S**	**I**		**S**	**I**
HR tube	8	9	HR tube	8	21	HR tube	0	0	HR tube	8	4
MS Billet	10	8	MS Billet	12	12	MS Billet	4	8	MS Billet	8	4
CR tube	15	15	CR tube	12	16	CR tube	5	21	CR tube	9	2
CR wire	15	0	CR wire	15	0	CR wire	6	15	CR wire	12	15
CR sheet	16	8	CR sheet	15	16	CR sheet	8	0	CR sheet	13	4
HR sheet	18	15	HR sheet	15	8	HR sheet	15	15	HR sheet	13	12
HS Billet	21	24	HS Billet	16	8	HS Billet	16	4	HS Billet	14	3
HR wire	24	26	HR wire	21	0	HR wire	18	2	HR wire	15	21
CR pipe	24	12	CR pipe	21	8	CR pipe	18	13	CR pipe	15	16
HR pipe	24	12	HR pipe	24	8	HR pipe	18	5	HR pipe	15	12
Total	175	129	**Total**	159	97	**Total**	108	83	**Total**	122	93

Median Sales for Q1:

$$\text{Median of a series} = \text{value of the } \left(\tfrac{n+1}{2}\right)^{\text{th}} \text{term}$$

Here, median sales for Q1 equals:

$$\text{Value of } \left(\tfrac{10+1}{2}\right)^{\text{th}} \text{product} = \text{value of the } 5.5^{\text{th}} \text{product}.$$

The value of the 5.5^{th} product equals

$$\text{Average of 16 \& 18} = (16 + 18)/2 = 17 \text{ MT}$$

Similarly, median sales for Q2, Q3, and Q3 are (15 + 15)/2 = 15, (8 + 23)/2 = 11.5, and (13 + 13)/2 = 13 MT, respectively. Hence, the statement is correct.

The answer for the part C is "Yes."

Example 3

The table gives data for three attributes of 16 brands of cars: 1) Performance, 2) Style, and 3) Value for money. Each attribute for a brand of car is rated out of 10 points by a group of experts. Total Score was computed as a weighted mean of three scores, using the same weights for each brand of cars.

Rank	Brand	Car company	Performance Score	Style Score	Value for money Score	Total Score
1	3 Series	BMW	9	9.1	8.8	9.00
2	7 Series	BMW	9.2	7.3	9.7	8.54
3	Expedition	Ford Motors	8.8	9	7	8.52
4	Sonata	Hyundai	9.3	7.5	9	8.52
5	Fiesta	Ford Motors	8	9	6.5	8.10
6	Juke	Nissan	7.1	9	6.4	7.72
7	Sonic	General Motors	8.3	7.7	5.9	7.58
8	5 Series	BMW	8.2	5.3	8.2	7.04
9	Grandeur	Hyundai	7	7.8	4.4	6.80
10	JM	Hyundai	7.2	6.8	4.7	6.54
11	Cruze	General Motors	6.6	5.6	5.5	5.98
12	M Model	BMW	5.5	6.4	5.5	5.86
13	Micra	Nissan	5.7	5.9	4.8	5.60
14	Maliba	General Motors	7.3	4.3	4.5	5.54
15	Dayz	Nissan	4.8	3.8	3.4	4.12
16	Mondeo	Ford Motors	4.1	4.8	2.2	4

For each of the following statements, select "Yes" if the statement is true based on the information provided; otherwise select "No".

	Yes	No	
A	○	○	Considering the median Style scores to compare Nissan and BMW cars, BMW cars are more stylish than Nissan cars.
B	○	○	The score for Performance and the score for Value-for-money had equal weights in the computation of the total score.
C	○	○	There is a positive correlation between the Performance score vs. the Value-for-money score.

Solution, Part A

The question asks you to compare the median style scores for BMW and Nissan cars. To get this, sort the table by column 3, Car company. This will group all BMWs and all Nissan cars.

Refer to the sorted table given below. Observe that the median style score for BMW, 6.85, is more than that for Nissan, 5.9.

Sorted by column 3

Col 3	Col 4	Col 5
Car company	Performance Score	**Style Score**
BMW	8.2	5.3
BMW	5.5	6.4
BMW	9.2	7.3
BMW	9	9.1
Ford Motors	4.1	4.8
Ford Motors	8.8	9
Ford Motors	8	9
General Motors	7.3	4.3
General Motors	6.6	5.6
General Motors	8.3	7.7
Hyundai	7.2	6.8
Hyundai	9.3	7.5
Hyundai	7	7.8
Nissan	4.8	**3.8**
Nissan	5.7	**5.9**
Nissan	7.1	**9**

Median Style scores for BMW

$$= \frac{2^{nd} \text{ value} + 3^{rd} \text{ value}}{2}$$

$$= \frac{6.4 + 7.3}{2} = 6.85$$

Median Style scores for Nissan

$$= 2^{nd} \text{ value} = 5.9$$

The answer for Part A is "Yes."

Solution, Part B

Let us first understand how the Total Score is calculated. Total Score is a weighted mean score (weighted average) of the three scores: Performance score (PS), Style score (SS), and Value-for-money (VFM) score. The question asks you to find out whether the weight of Performance and that of VFM are same in the computation of Total Score.

However, there is no information given about the Style score.

The optimum approach is to assume that the question statement is true i.e. *the weight of Performance and that of VFM are same.* Now you should calculate the weight of Style score at least twice from any two sets of scores while computing total score. If the values of weights for Style score are same, the answer is "Yes"; otherwise "No".

Say, the weights of Performance score = weights of the VFM score = 1, and the weights of the Style score = x.

Now, apply the formula of weighted mean.

$$\text{Weighted mean} = \frac{\text{PS weight} \times \text{PS} + \text{VFMS weight} \times \text{VFMS} + \text{SS weight} \times \text{SS}}{\text{total weight}};$$

where PS is the Performance score, VFMS is the VFM score, and SS is the Style score.

By plugging in the assumed values of weights in the formula, you get:

$$\text{Total score} = \frac{\text{PS} + \text{VFMS} + x \times \text{SS}}{(2 + x)}$$

To calculate x, plug in Style scores for any two brands of cars into the formula. If the values of x calculated from each set of data are not same, then the question statement is not true. Otherwise, try the same approach with one more brand of cars, to be doubly sure that the question statement is true.

Say, we take the 3-Series and Mondeo brand cars.

For the 3-Series brand, the scores for Performance, Style, VFM, and Total Scores are 9, 9.1, 8.8, and 9, respectively. Plug in these values into the formula of total score:

$$9 = \frac{(9 + 8.8 + 9.1x)}{(2 + x)} \Rightarrow 18 + 9x = 17.8 + 9.1x \Rightarrow 0.2 = 0.1x \Rightarrow x = 2.$$

Now, try the same with the Mondeo brand. You get:

$$4 = \frac{(4.1 + 2.2 + 4.8x)}{(2 + x)} \Rightarrow 8 + 4x = 6.3 + 4.8x \Rightarrow 1.7 = 0.8x \Rightarrow x = 2.125.$$

Since the values of x are not same ($x = 2$ or 2.125), hence the statement is false.

The answer for part B is "No".

For your curiosity, the ratio of weights of Performance score to that of VFM score to that of Style score is $2 : 2 : 1$.

Solution, Part C

This is a question on the concept of correlation. Hopefully, you have already gone through this concept in the book. Nevertheless, we repeat it:

> "Two entities are *positively correlated* if both of them either increase in tandem or decrease in tandem. Conversely, the entities are *negatively correlated* if the other entity decreases in value when the first entity increases in value, or vice versa. The two entities are not correlated if the increase or the decrease in the value of second entity cannot be concluded relative to the increase or the decrease in the value of first entity."

To approach this problem, sort the table by column 4, Performance score, so that the values are arranged in ascending order or, in other words, in the increasing trend.

The next step is to observe how the entity in column 6, Value for money Score, behaves. As you can observe in the sorted table given below, the downward-pointing arrows represent increasing values, while upward-pointing arrows represent decreasing values.

Sorted by column 4

Col 4	Col 5	Col 6
Performance Score	Style Score	**Value for money Score**
4.1	4.8	2.2
4.8	3.8	3.4
5.5	6.4	5.5
5.7	5.9	4.8
6.6	5.6	5.5
7	7.8	4.4
7.1	9	6.4
7.2	6.8	4.7
7.3	4.3	4.5
8	9	6.5
8.2	5.3	8.2
8.3	7.7	5.9
8.8	9	7
9	9.1	8.8
9.2	7.3	9.7
9.3	7.5	9

Looking at the arrows, you cannot conclude that these entities are perfectly correlated as there are many downward and many upward arrows. You must do some more analysis.

Again observing the arrows, you will find that the length of downward-pointing arrows is longer than that for upward-pointing arrows, which means that most values in the column 6 are increasing with the increase in the values in column 4, implying that the entities have, though not perfect, a strong positive correlation.

The answer for part C is "Yes."

Example 4

Cricket is played in a few select countries. Among these, Cricket is the most popular sport in a few of them. It is played in three formats: T20: played for four hours; One-Day: played for 8 hours; and Five-Day: played for 8 hours a day for five days.

The table given below presents percentage distribution of Cricket matches national teams played last year in three formats.

Country	Cricket-Most Popular sport?	T20	One-Day	Five-Day
Australia	No	65	28	7
Bangladesh	Yes	45	35	20
England	No	20	35	45
India	Yes	9	30	61
New Zealand	No	44	38	18
Pakistan	Yes	8	36	56
South Africa	No	66	10	24
Sri Lanka	Yes	4	35	61
West Indies	Yes	36	36	28
Zimbabwe	No	56	36	8

For each of the following statements, select *Would help explain* if were true, help explain some of the information in the table. Otherwise, select *Would not help explain*.

	Would help explain	Would not help explain	
A	○	○	Among its three formats, Cricket in its T20 format is more popular in the countries where Cricket is not their most popular sport than in countries where Cricket is their most popular sport.
B	○	○	Among the subcontinent countries: India, Pakistan, Sri Lanka, and Bangladesh, the One-Day format is the second most preferred type of Cricket format.
C	○	○	More Five-Day matches were played by each of India and Sri Lanka than by any other countries.

Solution, Part A

The question wants you to find out if more number of T20 Cricket matches are played than other two formats in the countries where Cricket is not the most popular sport than that in countries where it is the most popular sport.

To deduce this, you should sort the table by column 2, Popularity of Sport.

Sorted by column 2

Col1	Col2	Col3	Col4	Col5
Country	**Cricket-Most Popular sport?**	**T20**	**One-Day**	**Five-Day**
Australia	No	65	28	7
England	No	**20**	35	45
New Zealand	No	44	38	18
South Africa	No	66	10	24
Zimbabwe	No	56	36	8
Bangladesh	Yes	**45**	35	20
India	Yes	9	30	61
Pakistan	Yes	8	36	56
Sri Lanka	Yes	4	35	61
West Indies	Yes	**36**	**36**	28

You see in the table given above that for England, where Cricket is not the most popular sport, the least number of T20 matches are played than the two other formats. On the other hand, in the West Indies, where Cricket is the most popular sport, the T20 format is as popular as the One-Day format. Similarly, in Bangladesh, where Cricket is the most popular sport, the more number of T20 matches are played than the two other formats.

The analysis shows that the table does not help explain the statement.

The answer to part A is "Would not help explain".

Solution, Part B

The question wants you to determine whether for countries: India, Pakistan, Sri Lanka, and Bangladesh, the number of One-Day matches played in each country lies between the number of T20 matches and the number of Five-Day matches.

Sorted by column 2

Col1	Col2	Col3	Col4	Col5
Country	**Cricket-Most Popular sport?**	**T20**	**One-Day**	**Five-Day**
Australia	No	65	28	7
England	No	20	35	45
New Zealand	No	44	38	18
South Africa	No	66	10	24
Zimbabwe	No	56	36	8
Bangladesh	Yes	45	> 35 >	20
India	Yes	9	< 30 <	61
Pakistan	Yes	8	< 36 <	56
Sri Lanka	Yes	4	< 35 <	61
West Indies	Yes	36	36	28

Looking at the table given above, you can infer that for each of these four countries, the percentages of One-Day matches lies between that of T20 and that of Five-Day matches, implying that One-Day format is the second most preferred type of Cricket format in them.

Alternatively, we can infer that in these four countries, either T20 or Five-Day format is the most popular.

So the table helps explain the statement.

The answer to part B is "Would help explain".

Solution, Part C

The question wants you to find out if more number of Five-Day matches were played by each of India and by Sri Lanka than by any other countries.

This question seems relatively simple to deduce, but it is not so. The data given in the table is the percentage distribution of matches played by each country in three formats. You cannot deduce any information about the absolute number of matches each country played.

The table does not help explain the statement.

The answer to part C is "Would not help explain".

Example 5

Weston Private Limited produces and sells various brands of televisions for select categories of televisions. The data given in the table shows the Regional Production percentage share, its relative rank, the Regional Sales percentage shares, and its relative rank for the company's products relative to competitors' products in the corresponding television product category. No two companies share the same rank.

TV Product category	Production, Regional Share(%)	Production, Regional Rank	Sales, Regional Share(%)	Sales, Regional Rank
3D LCD	25	3	30	2
3D LED	45	1	55	1
B/W TV	21	3	12	5
FST	64	1	74	1
LCD	28	2	12	3
LED	13	4	10	4
Plasma	12	6	5	8
Smart TV	24	2	32	1

For each of the following statements, select "Would help explain", if it would, if true, help explain some of the information in the table; otherwise, select "Would not help explain".

	Would help explain	Would not help explain	
A	○	○	If Weston Private Limited produces more than one-fourth of the regional production of any category of televisions, then it gains one of the top two ranks for the production for that category of televisions.
B	○	○	No individual company produces more than 68% of the regional production for the LCD category of televisions.
C	○	○	If Weston Private Limited is ranked last in regional sales for the B/W TV category of televisions, then the first ranker would gain a minimum of 46% of the regional sales share.

Solution, Part A

The question asks it's true that if Weston produces more than 25% ($1/4^{th}$) of the TVs, then its production rank is either first or second.

Looking at the table, you will find that there are three categories of TVs for which the percentage production share of Weston is more than 25%: 3D LED has 45% of production share and is ranked 1; FST has 64% of production share and is ranked 1; and LCD has 28% of production share and is ranked 2.

Hence the table does help explain the statement.

The answer to part A is "Would help explain".

Solution, Part B

The question wants you to find out if no company produces more than 68% of LCD TVs.

In the LCD TV category, Weston is ranked second in production share with a production share of 28%. It means that the first ranker may command production share of up to 72% (100% − 28%). We should not assume that there must be more than two companies.

Hence the table does not help explain the statement.

The answer to part B is "Would not help explain".

Solution, Part C

The question wants you to find out if Weston is ranked last in the regional sales for B/W TV category, then the first ranker would gain a minimum of 46% regional sales share.

Currently, in B/W TV category, Weston is ranked fifth in the regional sales with a sales share of 12%. Weston's fifth rank is the last rank (given in the question statement), implying that other four competitors will share 88% sales (100% − 12%). So the first ranker will have more than 22% sales share as 88%/4 = 22% will rank all the competitors at same rank, which is incorrect.

Similarly, the first ranker will command less than 52% sales share because assuming that companies ranked from second to fourth, each have a minimum of a little over 12% sales share, so collectively they will have more than 48% share–as each rank cannot have equal sales share. So, the first ranker will gain less than 52% sales share [100% − (48% & more)].

Hence the table does not help explain the statement.

The answer to part C is "Would not help explain".

Example 6

A gym has to choose a health drink from among eight health drinks in the market. The health drinks are rated based on four criterion. For each of the criterion in the table, if the rating value for a drink is more than or equal to the median rating value for that category, it is considered a "favored drink" in that category. If a drink is favored in more than one criterion, it is considered "more favorable". A drink is considered "more favorable" than another drink if it is favored in more criterions than does the other drink.

Health Drink Brand	Vitamin B12 Rating (10)	Vitamin B6 Rating (5)	Vitamin B3 Rating (100)	Vitamin C Rating (10)
Booster+	3	3.2	34	4
Deli	6	2.2	47	7
Doz	6	3.8	74	7
Energy+	5	3.2	52	5
MegaPower	5	3.2	54	5
MusclePower	6	4.2	74	7
PowerBooster	5	3.2	54	6
Topper	4	4.2	48	5

For each of the following statements, select "Yes" if the statement is true based on the information provided; otherwise select "No".

	Yes	No	
A	○	○	No other drinks are more favored than PowerBooster and MusclePower.
B	○	○	Topper and Booster+ are not favored for any of the criterion.
C	○	○	There are at least three drinks that are favored for all the four criterion.

Solution, Part A

The question wants you to find out whether there is a drink more favored than PowerBooster and MusclePower.

Since the question involves finding out the favored drinks in each category, first find out the median values for each category. See the tables given below.

In the table given below, the cells containing qualifying values for each criterion are shaded.

Col 1	Col 2	Col 3	Col 4	Col 5
Health Drink Brand	**Vitamin B12 Rating (10)**	**Vitamin B6 Rating (5)**	**Vitamin B3 Rating (100)**	**Vitamin C Rating (10)**
Booster+	3	3.2	34	4
Topper	4	4.2	48	5
Energy+	5	3.2	52	5
MegaPower	5	3.2	54	5
PowerBooster (All 4)	**5**	**3.2**	**54**	**6**
Deli	6	2.2	47	7
Doz (All 4)	**6**	**3.8**	**74**	**7**
MusclePower (All 4)	**6**	**4.2**	**74**	**7**
Median	**5**	**3.2**	**53**	**5.5**

You can rank the health drinks the number of times they are favorable. In this table, you will find that PowerBooster and MusclePower are favored the maximum number of times (four). Although Doz is also favored an equal number of times, it is not favored *more* number of times than either PowerBooster or MusclePower.

The answer to part A is "Yes."

Solution, Part B

The question asks if it's true that Topper and Booster+ are not favored for any of the criterion.

Referring again to the given table, you will find that both Topper and Booster+ are favored once: for Vitamin B6.

The answer to part B is "No".

Solution, Part C

The question asks if there are at least three drinks favored for all criterion. We see that PowerBooster, MusclePower, and Doz are favored for all the four criterion.

The answer for part C is "Yes."

Chapter 4

Graphics Interpretation

4.1 Strategies and Concepts

As stated earlier, the Graphics Interpretation questions ask you about a chart, graph, diagram, or other visual form of information. It is vital that you learn how to read these.

4.1.1 Some Terminology

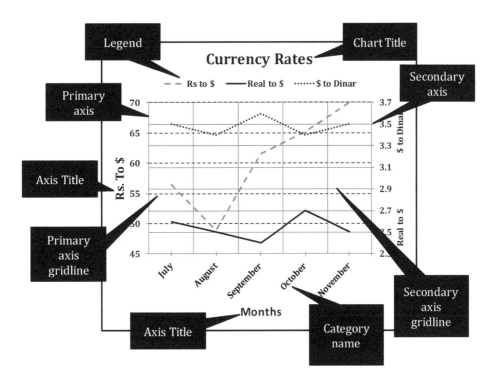

Figure 4.1: Key terms in graphs/charts.

- **Chart Titles**

  See the Figure 4.1 example chart. The chart title briefly describes what the graph is all about. Usually, it is a short phrase placed above the plot area of a graph.

- **Axis**

  There are two axes in Figure 4.1's the chart: the horizontal axis and the vertical axis. Few questions use charts with two vertical axes.

  - *Horizontal axis:*

    Horizontal axis usually shows categories such as years, months, cities, products, and so on.

  - *Vertical axis:*

    Vertical axis usually shows data-point values, such as population, inflation, number of cars, revenue, etc. Most often, the charts only have one vertical axis, on the chart's left. A few questions may use charts with two vertical axes. If so, the second vertical axis is on the chart's right. The left axis is called the *primary vertical axis* and the right one is called the *secondary vertical axis.*

- **Legends**

  Legends are the boxes on the right-hand-side, top, or bottom of the plot area. They indicate to which entity each bar or type of line relates.

- **Scale**

  Usually only one scale is used: the vertical-axis scale. A few questions may use two vertical scales. The vertical scale is marked with units (numerals) at equal intervals. For example, if a graph represents the number of students in certain schools, the vertical scale may be marked with 0, 50, 100, 150, 200, 250, and 300 units. So here, there are 50 units in each interval.

  A chart will use two vertical scales if two or more entities cannot be represented in the primary vertical axis. You must exercise caution while reading the values. For example, if a chart shows the number of students in some schools along with the percentage of passing students in those schools, the primary vertical axis may represent the number of students while the secondary vertical axis may represent the percentage passing.

  Pay attention to the legend and the question description so that you keep the primary and secondary axes correctly identified.

- **Gridlines**

  Horizontal and vertical gridlines make it easier to read the data. Vertical-axis gridlines extend up and Horizontal-axis gridlines extend across the plot area. Displayed for major and sometimes minor units, horizontal gridlines align with major and minor tick marks on the axis.

  You cannot display gridlines for the graphs that do not display axes, such as pie charts.

4.1.2 How to Read a Chart

You need not try to extract an EXACT value of data from a chart/graph. Your best estimate will do. For example, in Figure 4.2, the Rs./$ rate was approximately 57 in July, and the $/Dinar rate was approximately 3.6 in September. Don't worry about the values being just approximations, the options will be wide enough apart.

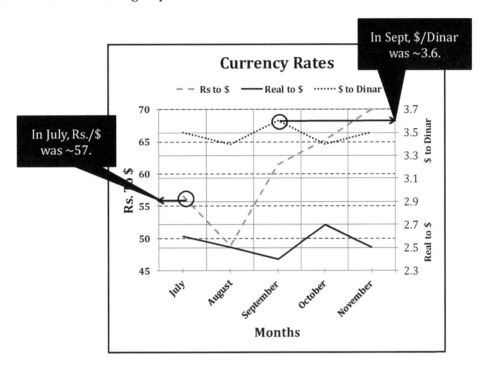

Figure 4.2: How to read a graph/chart.

Be careful to choose the appropriate vertical scale while reading the values of Rs./$ (on the primary vertical axis) and $/Dinar (on the secondary vertical axis).

4.2   Quantitative Concepts Tested in the Graphics Interpretation

- **Absolute increase or decrease**

  This is the simplest of all. You simply read the values of two or more data points and figure out the difference. **A word of caution**: Distinguish Absolute increase or decrease vs. Percentage increase or decrease.

- **Percentage increase or decrease**

  Suppose you are asked to calculate a percent value. Say, for example, you are asked:

  For a city whose population rose from 45 million in the year 2011 to 50 million in the year 2012, the percentage increase in the population would be _____%.

$$\% \text{ increase} = \left[\frac{(\text{new value} - \text{base value})}{\text{base value}} \right] \times 100\%$$

$$\Rightarrow \% \text{ increase in population} = \left[\frac{\text{population in 2012} - \text{population in 2011}}{\text{population in 2011}} \right] \times 100\%$$

$$\Rightarrow \% \text{ increase in population} = \frac{50 - 45}{45} \times 100\% = \frac{5}{45} \times 100\% = 11.11\%$$

- **Beware of the Word "than"**

  o If a question asks:

  By what percent is the population in the year 2011 less *than* the population in the year 2012?

  Will the answer be 11.11%? No. It is not. In this question, the base of comparison is changed to the year 2012, so year 2012 will appear in the denominator as the base value:

$$\% \text{ decrease in population } = \frac{50 - 45}{50} \times 100\% = \frac{5}{50} \times 100\% = 10\%$$

- **It's Not Always Percentage Increase or Decrease**

  o If the question asks:

  What percent is the population in the year 2011 of the population in the year 2012?

  You need not calculate the percentage increase or decrease. The answer would be calculated as given below:

$$\% = \frac{\text{population in 2011}}{\text{population in 2012}} \times 100\% = \frac{45}{50} \times 100\% = 90\%$$

- If the question asks:

    What percent is the population in the year 2012 of the population in the year 2011?

    You should calculate the same in the following way:

    $$\% = \frac{\text{population in 2012}}{\text{population in 2011}} \times 100\% = \frac{50}{45} \times 100\% = 111.11\%$$

- **Determine Increased or Decreased Value**

    - If the question asks:

        What would be the population in the year 2013 if the population grows at the same rate as it did during the period 2011–2012?

        You have already calculated the percentage increase in the population = 11.11%. Applying the traditional approach to solving this question is time-consuming. In the traditional approach, you would calculate the increase first, and then add the increase to the population in the year 2012 to get the population for the year 2013.

        The following approach will save your precious time:

        $$\text{population}|_{2013} = \text{population}|_{2012} \times (1 + \% \text{ increase})$$
        $$= 50 \times (1 + 11.11\%) = 50 \times (1 + 0.111) = 55.55 \text{ million}$$

    - Similarly, if the question is:

        What would be company X's revenue for next year if it decreased by 23.87% from the current year's revenue of \$237.48 million?

        The following approach will save your precious time:

        $$\text{revenue}|_{\text{next year}} = 237.48 \times (1 - 0.2387) = 237.48 \times 0.7613 = \$180.80 \text{ million}$$

        You can even save more time by truncating the decimals:

        $$\Rightarrow \text{revenue}|_{\text{next year}} = 237 \times (1 - 0.24) = 237 \times 0.76 \cong \$180 \text{ million}$$

    - If the question asks:

        A shopkeeper used to charge 15% margin on his products. Due to competition, he revised the margin to 10%. By what percent did the shopkeeper decrease his margin?

        The answer is certainly not 5%. It would rather be:

        $$\% \text{ decrease in margin} = \frac{15\% - 10\%}{15\%} \times 100\% = 33.33\%$$

        So, what does $15\% - 10\%$ represent?

        $$\text{Percent} - \text{Percent} = \text{Percent Point}$$

So, alternatively, you can also say that the shopkeeper reduced his margin by 5 percent points.

Remember,

$$percent - percent \neq percent$$

- **Percent of What?**

    ○ If the question asks:

    If 80% of students from a school play soccer and 25% of those joined a professional soccer club, what percentage of total students from the school did not join the club?

The answer is not 75% (100% − 25%).

You must pay attention to the verbiage. It is not always the case that the answer is a percentage of the total.

Here, the number of students who joined the club = 25% of 80% = 20%. So, if 20% of total students joined the club, 80% of total students did not join the club.

- **Trend Lines**

Scatterplots are tested in the GMAT-IR section. In scatterplots, data points are represented as dots, and these dots are usually many in number. A trend line is a straight line that tries to best fit or represent the scattered dots. See Figure 4.3 below.

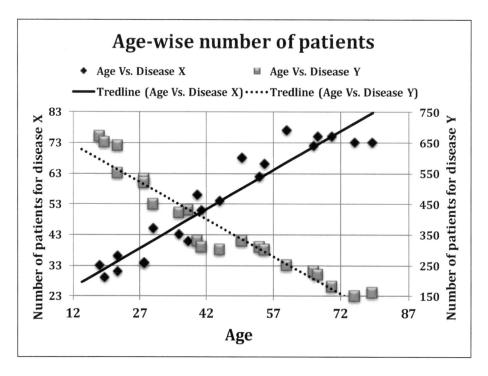

Figure 4.3: Scatter plot and Trend lines

Trend lines have slopes. If the slope moves up from bottom-left to top-right, it is called a "positive slope"; whereas if it moves from top-left to bottom-right, it is called a "negative slope."

- **Correlation**

  We have seen Correlation in Table Analysis, but it is tested in GI too, so we reproduce its definition again.

  Correlationis a measure of relationships between any two entities. Two entities are positively correlated if both of them either increase in tandem or decrease in tandem, whereas the entities are negatively correlated if one entity decreases in value while the other entity increases in value, or vice versa. The entities are not correlated if the increase or decrease in the value of one entity cannot be concluded relative to the increase or decrease in the value of the other.

  The Figure 4.4 shows the types and degrees of correlation.

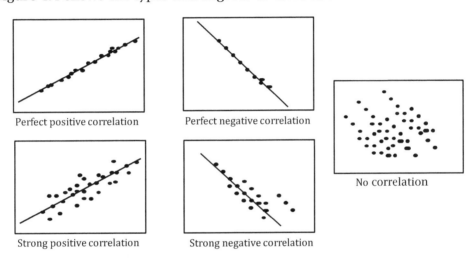

Figure 4.4: Degrees of Correlation

- **Probability**

  ○ *Basic Probability*

  As with Quants, the IR section also tests probability. The questions on probability are based on the very basic concept of probability.

  $$\text{Probability}(\text{Event } A) = \frac{\text{Number of occurrences of event } A}{\text{Number of occurrence of all events}}$$

  You must understand the meaning of "all events". It is not always "all the possible events" in the question, rather it is "all the *qualifying* events".

  So, if a question asks:

  What is the probability of selecting a boy out of 10 boys, 20 girls, 3 male teachers, and 2 female teachers; given that, in a single drawing, the selection is to be made out of a set of only males?

  $$\text{P}(\text{Boys}) = \frac{10}{10 + 3} = \frac{10}{13}$$

- *Going Other Way Around*

  Sometimes it is more time-consuming to calculate the **probability of an event to occur**. In that case, it may be more convenient to calculate the **probability of the event not to occur** and then deduce the probability of the event to occur.

  Here is how:

  P(event occurs) + P(event does not occur) = 1

  $\Rightarrow$ P(event occurs) = 1 − P(event does not occur)

  If the question asks:

  What is the probability of getting a yellow or green or red ball in a single draw out of 5 yellow, 3 green, 4 red, and 2 black balls?

  Instead of calculating the probability of getting a yellow or green or red ball, it is better to calculate the probability of getting a black ball and then deduct the calculated answer from 1.

  $$P(\text{Black}) = \frac{2}{(5 + 3 + 4 + 2)} = \frac{2}{14} = \frac{1}{7}$$

  $$\Rightarrow P(\text{Yellow or Green or Red}) = 1 - \frac{1}{7} = \frac{6}{7}$$

4.3 Process of Solving GI Questions

(1) *Understand the data set*

Read the question narration and the elements of graph. Understand the relationship of each element to the others. Sometimes legends are not given in the plot area. However, you can get information from the question narration or some notes given outside the plot area.

(2) *Understand the question*

As you know, that there are two Fill-In-the-Blank questions in a GI dataset. You have to select the best option from a drop-down menu. Remember that there is no partial credit for correct responses. Both responses must be correct to get the credit for the question.

Read the statement and stop to understand it. Mentally rephrase what is asked.

(3) *Develop an approach*

There could be two ways to approach a question. Most GI questions ask for a value in a statement to be filled in. However, it is not necessary to actually calculate values every single time. Even a logical approach can work and save your time.

(4) *Apply the approach*

Apply the approach you developed in previous step and select the correct option. Jot down the results of the calculations, as it is likely that the results in previous question may be required for intermediary steps in the question that follows.

4.4 Examples

Let us see some GMAT-like questions now. In an actual GMAT exam, you will have to select an option in a drop-down menu, but in this book, we have just listed the options.

Example 1

The bar graph shows the number of unemployed youth in a country for seven years.

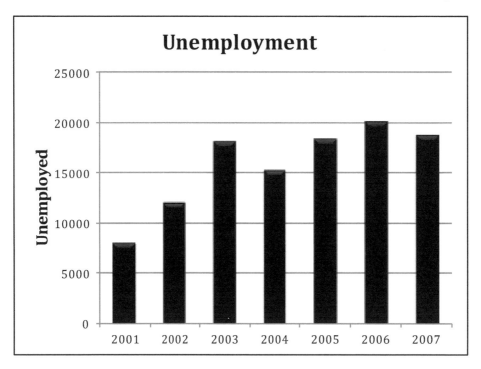

Based on the given information, use the drop-down menu to most accurately complete the following statements:

(A) The greatest increase in the number of unemployed youth from any year to its succeeding year is approximately _____.

    (A) 3736

    (B) 4152

    (C) 6108

    (D) 7542

(B) The number of unemployed youth in the year 2004 is approximately _____ percent of the number of unemployed youth in the year 2003.

    (A) 16

    (B) 19.5

    (C) 84

    (D) 119.5

Solution—Part A

The question asks you to determine the greatest absolute increase in the number of unemployed from any year to its succeeding year.

Clearly, the answer would be one of the following years; 2001-2002, 2002-2003, 2004-2005, and 2005-2006, as during the years 2003-2004, and 2006-2007, number of unemployed youths in fact decreased.

It is not advisable to calculate the increase for all four probable years. So, which year would have the maximum increase? Clearly, looking at the graph, you can see that the answer would be one of years between 2001-2002 and 2002-2003, because these two years have the highest jump over their previous year.

You see that the number of unemployed youths in the year 2001 is approximately 8000. You need not be very precise. Read the value to your best of capability. Similarly, the number of unemployed youths in the year 2002 is approximately 12000. The increase for the period 2001-2002 would be approximately 4000 ($\approx 12000 - \approx 8000$). Likewise, for the period 2002-2003, the increase would be approximately 6000 ($\approx 18000 - \approx 12000$). It is clear that the answer would be ≈ 6000. The closest option is C, 6108.

The correct answer is option C.

Solution—Part B

Let the number of unemployed youth in the year 2004 = $x\%$ of unemployed youth in the year 2003. You are supposed to calculate x.

Reading from the graph, you find that

$$\text{unemployed}_{2004} = 15000 \quad \text{and} \quad \text{unemployed}_{2003} = 18000.$$

Hence,

$$x = \left(\frac{15000}{18000}\right) \times 100\% = 83.33\%.$$

The closest answer is 84%.

You must pay attention to the verbiage. The question does not ask you for percentage increase or decrease. Had you made that mistake, the options A and B were the traps laid down for you. Similarly, swapping 2003 with 2004 would also get you in trouble. Option D was another trap: $(18000/15000) \times 100\% = 119.50\%$.

The correct answer is option C.

Example 2

The Venn diagram represents information about a group of 75 executives. The executives read either one, two or all of the three newspapers: *The Economics Times, The Wall Street Journal,* and *Business Week.*

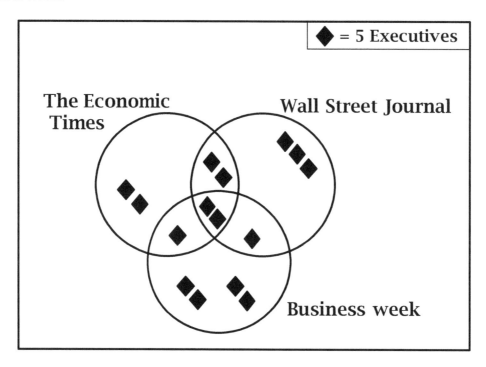

Based on the given information, use the drop-down menus to most accurately complete the following statements:

(A) An executive is randomly picked from a selected group of executives. The probability that the executive reads only *Business Week* given that the selected group reads either *Business Week* or *The Wall Street Journal* or both is _____.

    (A) 0.27

    (B) 0.31

    (C) 0.50

    (D) 0.87

(B) An executive is randomly picked from the group. The probability that the executive reads *Business Week* or *The Economic Times,* but not *The Wall Street Journal* is _____.

    (A) 1/15

    (B) 1/5

    (C) 7/15

    (D) 4/5

Solution—Part A

You are to calculate the probability of selecting an executive who reads ONLY *Business Week* among all the executives who read either *Business Week* or *The Wall Street Journal*, or both.

$$\text{P(Only } BW) = \frac{\text{Number of executives who read only } BW}{\text{Number of executives who read } BW + WSJ - \text{both}} = \frac{4}{15-2} = \frac{4}{13} = 0.31.$$

See the figure given below.

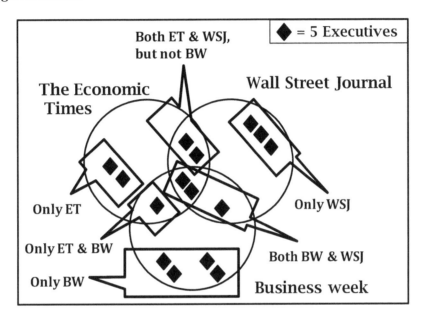

The correct answer is option B.

The value of "number of executives who read $BW + WSJ - $ both" alternatively could have been calculated as $8 + 8 - 3 = 13$, but that would be a lengthy calculation. We ignored the information that one rhombus equals five executives, as it would have no impact on the calculation. Multiplication by 5 in both the numerator and the denominator would have been cancelled out.

Solution—Part B

You are to calculate the probability of selecting an executive who reads anything except the *WSJ*. The optimum approach would be to calculate the probability of selecting an executive who reads the *WSJ*, and then deducting that value from 1:

$$\text{P(only } ET + \text{only } BW + \text{both)} = 1 - \text{P}(WSJ) = 1 - \tfrac{8}{15} = \tfrac{7}{15}.$$

The correct answer is option C.

Example 3

The bubble diagram represents the performance of a Blue-Chip company. Its 6-year performance is represented by six bubbles. Each bubble represents the ratio of revenue-to-profit. (The figures are mentioned on the bubbles.) The horizontal axis represents profit ($K), and the vertical axis, years of performance. The relative position of a bubble's center point indicates profit on the X-axis, and the year of occurrence on the Y-axis.

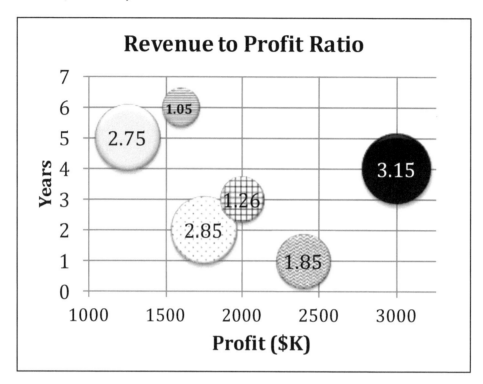

Based on the given information, use the drop-down menus to most accurately complete the following statements:

(A) The least amount of expense observed in any year during a 6-year period is $_____.

    (A) 80K

    (B) 520K

    (C) 1250K

    (D) 1600K

(B) The profit-to-expense ratio is the least for the year _____.

    (A) 1

    (B) 2

    (C) 3

    (D) 4

    (E) 5

    (F) 6

Solution—Part A and B

Understand the bubble chart first. You can get three data from it:

(1) *Profit*: the X-axis value of a bubble's center

(2) *Year of occurrence*: the Y-axis value of a bubble's center

(3) *Ratio of revenue to profit*: the number mentioned on a bubble

For part A, you have to find the least expense in any year of the 6-year period. Information about expenses are not given in the graph. You can apply common knowledge here.

You know that:

$$\text{Expense} = \text{Revenue} - \text{Profit}$$

Using this, you can find the value of the expense-to-profit ratio.

For example, for Year 1, revenue/profit = 1.85 or 1.85/1. For ratio purposes, you can assume that revenue = 1.85, and profit = 1. This will give expense = 1.85 − 1 = 0.85. Or, the expense-profit ratio is 0.85/1 = 0.85.

Similarly, you can calculate the values of the expense-profit ratio for all the years. The values for expense-profit ratios for all six years would be 0.85, 1.85, 0.26, 2.15, 1.75, and 0.05, respectively.

For part B, you have to find out the year for which the profit-expense ratio is the least. The correct answer would be the year for which expense-profit ratio is the highest. Referring to the the calculated figures for expense-profit ratios (given above), you will find that the expense-profit ratio is highest for Year 4; it equals 2.15.

Hence, option D is the correct answer for part B of the question.

Coming back to part A of the question, you have to find out the value of least expense that occurred in any year of the 6-year period. You already know the value of expense-profit ratio.

Hence,

$$\text{Expense} = (\text{Expense-to-Profit ratio}) \times \text{Profit}$$

To get the least value of expense, the ideal year would be one that has the lowest value for its expense-profit ratio, as well as its profit. Low values for the expense-profit ratio are for the years 1, 3, and 6, while low values for profit are for the years 5, and 6. Clearly, the expenses for year 6 is the answer for part A of the question. The expenses for year 6 = 0.05 × profit. We see that the approximate value of profit for year 6 = $1600K; thus he expenses for year 6 = 0.05 × 1600 = $80K.

If you are curious, here are the values of expenses for all six years:

Year	1	2	3	4	5	6
Expense-to-Profit Ratio	0.85	1.85	0.26	2.15	1.75	0.05
Profit ($K)	≈ 2400	1750	2000	3000	1250	≈ 1600
Expense ($K) = (Expense-Profit ratio) × Profit	≈ 2040	3238	520	6450	2188	≈ **80**

Hence, option A is the correct answer for part A of the question.

Example 4

In a town P, the natives are affected by two rare diseases X and Y. In the following scatterplot, there are two sets of 21 points arranged vertically: one represents the comparison of age to the number of patients of disease-X (black rhombus), and the other represents the comparison of age to the number of patients of disease-Y (grey squares).

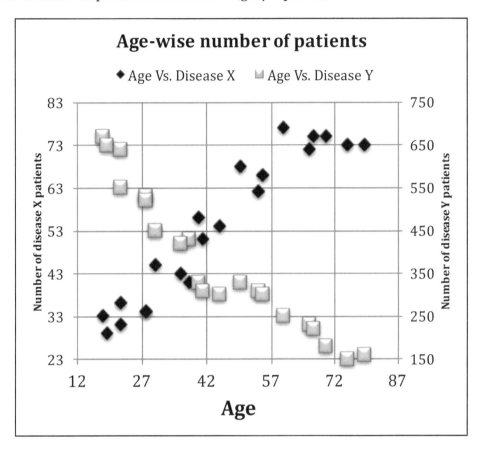

Based on the given information, use the drop-down menus to most accurately complete the following statements:

(A) The lowest number of patients for disease X lie in the between age group _____.

    (A) 12 and 27

    (B) 27 and 42

    (C) 42 and 57

    (D) 57 and 72

    (E) 72 and 87

(B) The correlation between the patients of disease X and those of disease Y is _____.

    (A) a strong positive

    (B) a strong negative

    (C) negligible

Solution—Part A

You have to find the age group for which the total number of patients with disease X (black rhombus) is the least. If you did not pay attention to details, you may do this seemingly easy question wrong. Remember that the weight for each rhombus is different. The more you go up the Y-axis, the higher the weight of a rhombus is. It means that two rhombuses lying between the 72–87 age group collectively may weigh more than the four rhombuses lying between the 12–27 age group.

Had you attempted this question hurriedly, you would have marked option E as the correct answer.

How do you approach this question? Should you read the value of the weight for each rhombus, add them for each age group and compare the total? Answer is "No". You cannot afford to do this in the limited amount of time. GMAT never throws you a question that involves a lot of calculation. Even if you have the luxury of using the calculator provided in the IR section, it is not a wise approach to do the computation involving 21 values.

This question demands a logical approach. It is clear that the answer would NOT be among age groups: 27–42, 42–57, or 57–72 since each age group has either 4 or 6 rhombuses. Comparing these age groups with the 12–27 age group, you can safely infer that number of patients for the 12–27 age group would be the least as the age group 12–27 also has 4 rhombuses. Note that rhombuses lying in age group 12–27 represent relatively less number of patients than the ones lying in age groups: 27–42, 42–57, or 57–72.

So, you have only two contenders: the 12–27 and the 72–87 age groups. Now must you calculate values now? Well, not really. You can estimate that the average value for the four rhombuses lying in the 12–27 age group is around 33. So, the total number of patients for the 12–27 age group $\approx 33 \times 4 \approx 132$. As far as the total number of patients for the 72–87 age group is concerned, it is $73 + 73 = 146$. Clearly, the number of patients for 12–27 age group is the least in value.

The correct answer is option A.

Solution—Part B

We assume that you have gone through the theory part of correlation. Now, how do you approach this question? Look at the image given below.

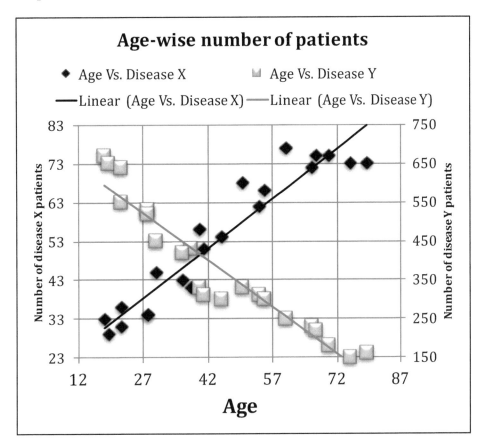

First, imagine a trend line that is the best fit for all the black rhombuses. Similarly, do the same for the grey squares. You will observe that the trend line for disease *X* has a positive slope (that is, it moves up from bottom-left to top-right), while that for disease *Y* has a negative slope (that is, it moves down from top-left to bottom-right). Which means that while the number of patients for disease *X* increases with the age, it decreases for disease *Y*, implying a *strong negative correlation*.

The correct answer is option B.

Example 5

The chart given below shows a corporate strategy map of a customer services company. The arrows connecting the ovals show how various entities are interconnected at the company level.

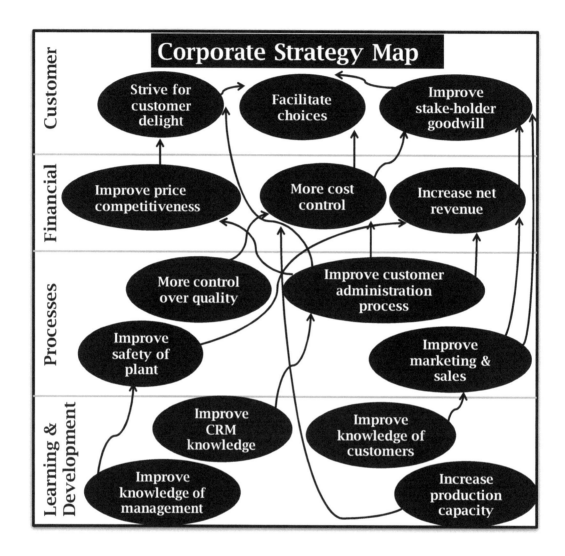

Based on the given information, use the drop-down menus to most accurately complete the following statements:

(A) If the company cannot 'Increase production capacity', it can still achieve 'More control over cost' by _____.

    (A) improving knowledge of management

    (B) facilitating more choices

    (C) improving marketing and sales

    (D) improving CRM knowledge

(B) By improving _____, company can enhance 'Customer delight'.

    (A) Production capacity

    (B) Marketing and sales

    (C) CRM knowledge

    (D) Stakeholder's goodwill

Solution–Part A

The given chart is called a "Strategy map" or a "Visual chart." In this chart, one activity leads to one or more activities represented by the arrows.

In part A of the question:

> If the company cannot 'Increase production capacity', it can still achieve 'More control over cost' by_____.

Your objective is to achieve 'More control over cost', but the constraint is that the company cannot 'Increase production capacity'.

- *Objective*: achieve 'More control over cost'.

- *Constraint*: the company cannot 'Increase production capacity'.

Let us analyze each option.

(A) 'Improving knowledge of management' leads to 'Improving safety of plants', which leads to 'Improvement in net revenue'. However, this does not lead to the objective of achieving 'More control over cost'.

(B) The objective of achieving 'More control over cost' leads to 'Facilitating more choices', not vice-versa.

(C) 'Improving marketing and sales' leads to two activities:

    (a) 'Increasing net revenue' (but this does not lead to 'More control over cost')

    (b) 'Improving the stake holder's goodwill' (but this does not lead to 'More control over cost')

(D) 'Improving CRM knowledge' leads to 'Improving the customer administration process', which leads to the objective: 'More control over cost'. This is the correct answer.

The correct answer is option D.

Solution—Part B

Objective: 'Enhance customer delight'

Let us analyze each option:

(A) 'Improving production capacity' does not lead to the objective of 'Enhancing customer delight'.

(B) 'Improving marketing and sales' leads to two activities:

　　(a) 'Increasing net revenue'; but this does not lead to the objective of 'Enhancing customer delight'.

　　(b) 'Improving stake holder's goodwill'; but again, this does not lead to the objective of 'Enhancing customer delight'.

(C) 'Improving CRM knowledge' leads to improving the 'Customer administration process', which leads to the objective: 'More control over cost'. This is the correct answer.

The correct answer is option C.

Example 6

The PE Corporation has four warehouses that stock electric bulbs. The line-graph presents the number of cartons stocked by the first two warehouses, and an average stock of all the four warehouses for the months September to June.

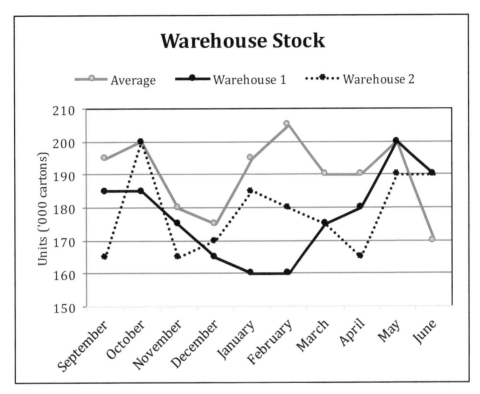

Based on the given information, use the drop-down menus to most accurately complete the following statements:

   (A) The highest number of electric bulb cartons stocked by the other two warehouses (warehouse 3 and 4) was in _____.

   (A) October

   (B) December

   (C) February

   (D) February and in May

   (E) May

   (B) The lowest number of electric bulb cartons stocked by the other two warehouses (warehouse 3 and 4) was in _____.

   (A) November

   (B) December

   (C) December and in May

   (D) May

   (E) June

Solution—Part A

Let us understand the question. The PE Corporation has four warehouses. In the graph, the black line represents stocks for Warehouse 1, the dashed-line for Warehouse 2, and the grey line for the averages of all the four warehouses.

Note there is no information about Warehouses 3 and 4. However, you still can find information about their stocks.

As you know,

$$\text{Stocks for WH 3 + WH 4 = Total stocks of all 4 warehouses}$$
$$- \text{(Sum of WH 1 and WH 2 stocks)}$$

$$\Rightarrow \text{Stocks for WH 3 + WH 4 = 4} \times \text{Average stock of all 4 warehouses}$$
$$- \text{(Sum of WH 1 and WH 2 stocks)}$$

Look at the first part of the question:

The highest number of electric bulb cartons stocked by the other two warehouses (warehouse 3 and 4) was in _____.

Looking at the equation, you can deduce that

$$\text{WH 3 and WH 4 stocks = 4} \times \text{average stock} - \text{WH 1 stock} - \text{WH 2 stock.}$$

You can infer that to get the highest value for WH 3 and WH 4 stocks, the average stock value must be the highest, as it would increase their values, whereas the WH 1 and WH 2 stocks should be the lowest, as these otherwise would decrease their values to a minimum.

Instead of calculating the values for WH 3 and WH 4 stocks for all the given months in the options, you can analyze the options by observing the graph.

Month	Value of Average Stock (Ideal – Highest)	Value of WH 1 stock (Ideal – Lowest)	Value of WH 2 stock (Ideal – Lowest)	Remarks
October	*Too high* (Positive for WH 3 and WH 4 to be highest)	*High* (Negative for WH 3 and WH 4 to be highest)	*Highest* (Most negative for WH 3 and WH 4 to be highest)	October cannot be the answer, as the two factors are negative.
December	*Too low* (Negative for WH 3 and WH 4 to be highest)	*Too low* (Positive for WH 3 and WH 4 to be highest)	*Too low* (Positive for WH 3 and WH 4 to be highest)	December can be eliminated as compared to February. It still has one negative factor.
February	*Highest* (Most positive for WH 3 and WH 4 to be highest)	*Lowest* (Most positive for WH 3 and WH 4 to be highest)	*Mid-way* (Neutral)	February is the **correct** answer. Out of three factors, two are the most positive, while the third one is neutral.
May	*Too high* (Positive for WH 3 and WH 4 to be highest)	*Highest* (Most negative for WH 3 and WH 4 to be highest)	*Too high* (Negative for WH 3 and WH 4 to be highest)	May cannot be the answer, as the two factors are negative.

So, the correct answer is C.

If you are curious, here are the stocks for all months.

WH 3 and WH 4 stocks for Feb. $= 4 \times 205 - 160 - 180 = 820 - 340 = 480$.

Similarly, WH 3 and WH 4 stocks for October, December, and May months are: 415, 365, and 410, respectively.

The following image can help you understand how to do the above analysis mentally.

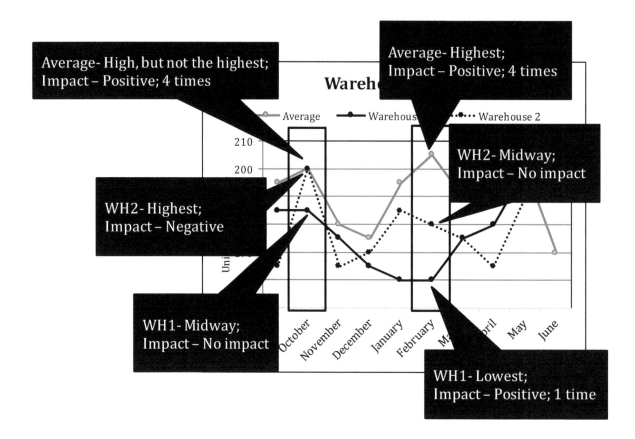

Solution—Part B

Look at the first part of the question:

> The lowest number of electric bulb cartons stocked by the other two warehouses (warehouse 3 and 4) was in _____.

This is a similar question to the previous one. You have to find the month that stocked the *lowest* number of cartons in WH 3 and WH 4, instead of the highest.

The strategy would be opposite of what you applied in the previous question.

Looking again at:

> WH 3 and WH 4 stocks = 4 × average stock − WH 1 stock − WH 2 stock,

you can infer that to get the lowest values for WH 3 and WH 4, the average stock must be the lowest, as that would decrease the values, whereas WH 1 and WH 2 stocks should be the highest, as those, too, would decrease the values.

Inferring the probable values for the option months—November, December, May, and June—you can infer that June is the answer, as the average stocks for June is the lowest of all the months, while the stocks for WH 1 and WH 2 are high.

So, the correct answer is E.

If you are curious, here are the stocks for all months.

WH 3 and WH 4 stocks for June = $4 \times 170 - 190 - 190 = 680 - 380 = 300$.

Similarly, the values for November, December, and May are: 380, 365, and 410, respectively.

Take Away: Remember that if the average stock is the most positive for a month, its effect is four times that of each of WH 1 and WH 2 stocks.

Have a look at the following figure for more clarity.

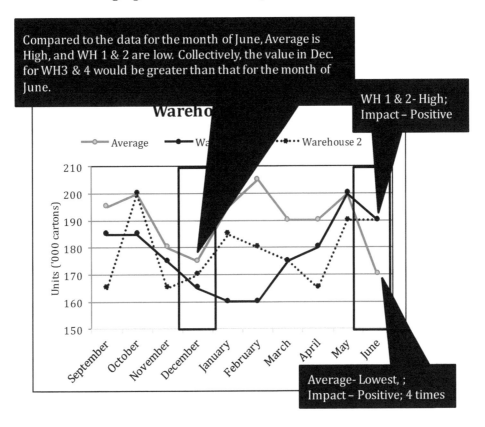

Example 7

The bar chart shows the percentage distribution of expenditures for three families: *A*, *B*, and *C*, on the primary vertical axis. The expenditure is categorized into four categories: food, clothing, home, and entertainment. In addition, the expenditures of individual families represented by line graph are plotted (in dollars) on the secondary vertical axis.

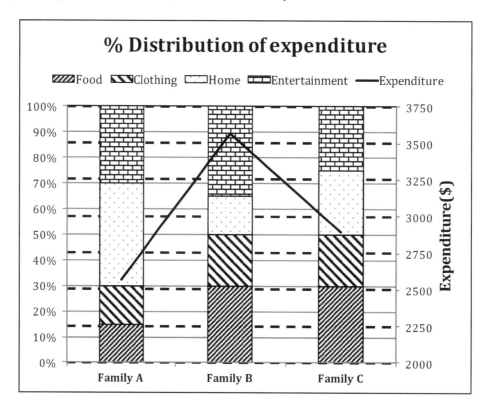

Based on the given information, use the drop-down menus to most accurately complete the following statements:

(A) Family *A* needs to decrease its expenditure on their home by _____ to match that of family *B*.

    (A) 25.00%

    (B) 28.11%

    (C) 47.84%

    (D) 62.50%

(B) _____ does not spend the most among the three families in any of the four categories.

    (A) Family *A*

    (B) Family *B*

    (C) Family *C*

Solution—Part A

The expenditure on its home by a family would be given by the product of percentage expenditure on its home × expenditure (in dollars).

Expenditure on its home by family A = 40% × (≈ 2500) = \$1000.
Expenditure on its home by family B = 15% × (≈ 3600) = \$540.

The percentage decrement in expenditure on its home by family A to match that by family B equals:

$$\frac{\text{Expenditure by family } A - \text{Expenditure by family } B}{\text{Expenditure by family } A} \times 100\% = \frac{(1000 - 540)}{1000} \times 100\% \approx 46\%.$$

The closest option is 47.85%.

The correct answer is C.

Solution—Part B

The question wants you to find a family that does not spend the most in any of the categories: food, home, clothing, and entertainment.

Looking at the graph above, you see that there is only one family that does not spend the most in any category. Observe that family B has the highest expenditures among all three families, and for entertainment, it spends the most (35%). Since family B spends the most in at least in one category, option B is ruled out as an answer, and the correct one is between families A and C.

In Part A of the question, you have already calculated how much family A spends on its home. Its expenditure (\$1000) is more than that for family B (\$540). You should also calculate the figure for family C. Expenditure on its home by family C = 25% × ≈ 2900 =$\approx$ \$725. So we conclude that family A spends the most in the home category.

This implies that the correct answer must be family C.

The correct answer is option C.

Example 8

The graph given below shows 60-monthly data for the mean deviation of Brazilian currency, the Real, observed for the years 2008–2013. The mean deviation of the Real is measured by the current month's rate vs. the U.S. Dollar less the five-year mean rate vs. the U.S. Dollar. The graph also shows a line of best fit for the data points.

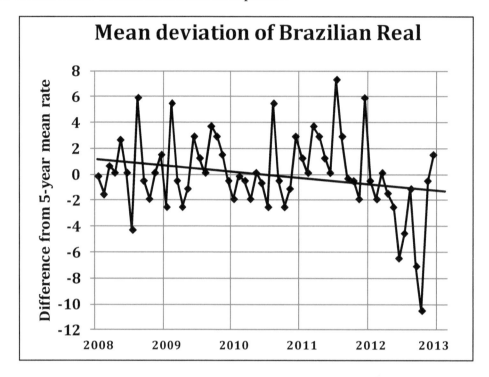

Based on the given information, use the drop-down menus to most accurately complete the following statements:

(A) To conclude that mean value of the Brazilian Real is decreasing in the international market, it would be helpful to see a more comprehensive graph of the same period that shows _____.

   (A) weeks on the horizontal axis

   (B) a broader range for the vertical axis

   (C) a similar graph for the mean deviation of the Brazilian Real versus other popular currencies in the international market

   (D) a similar graph for the mean deviation of the U.S. Dollar versus the Brazilian Real

(B) The conclusion that the mean value of Brazilian Real has decreased over the years would be most strengthened if the set of measurements in the year _____ were revised towards the current line of best fit.

   (A) 2008

   (B) 2009

   (C) 2010

   (D) 2011

   (E) 2012

Solution—Part A

What does it mean that the mean value of Brazilian Real is decreasing in the international market? The questions wants you to make sure that the Real is depreciating in the international market. The graph shows the mean deviation of the Real only versus U.S. Dollar currency. The trend line or the current line of best fit for mean deviation shows that the slope is negative—implying that the mean value of the Real is decreasing in the international market.

(A) Having a more comprehensive graph of the same period that shows weeks on the horizontal axis would not help, as it would not impact the trend line. The 60 data points plotted on the graph would not be impacted, either.

(B) By the similar reasoning as in option A, seeing the more comprehensive graph of the same period that shows broader range for the vertical axis would not help, as it would not impact the trend line.

(C) It could be possible that the Real is not devaluating, but the U.S. Dollar is appreciating because of a reviving U.S. economy. So, seeing a similar graph for the mean deviation of Brazilian Real versus other popular currencies in the international market would make sure the Real is decreasing.

(D) A similar graph for the mean deviation of the U.S. Dollar versus the Real is nothing but the same graph with inverted values. It does not provide any additional information.

The correct answer is option C.

Solution—Part B

First, understand the meaning of the question: it wants you to verify the claim that the mean value of the Brazilian Real has decreased over the years. The trend line has a negative slope, but it is not very pronounced. Had the slope been more steep, you could have safely concluded that the Real had been decreasing in value.

So, to strengthen the claim, you must increase the magnitude of the slope of trend line. How do you do this? Well, you should bring up the data-points above the trend line closer to itself.

The years 2008, 2010, and 2012 have a good number of points below the trend line. Bringing these data points closer to the trend line would rather decrease the magnitude of its negative slope, but you do not want this.

Since you can alter the data points for ONLY one year (see the options), you must choose the year whose collective deviation of 12 data points is more than that of others. Both the years 2009 and 2011 have data points lying significantly above the trend line. You would observe that the year 2011 was the best year in terms of the economy as the mean deviations for as many as seven months were positive (seven rhombuses are above the major grid-line of "0"), and negative for only three months (three rhombuses are below the major grid-line of "0"). If you move these points toward the trend line, it would strengthen the claim that the Real has decreased over the years.

Currently, more data points of the year 2011 than of the year 2009 are working against your goal—Brazilian Real has decreased over the years—so moving the data points of 2009 though would also strengthen the claim, it would not be to the extent the data points of year 2011 would do.

The correct answer is option D.

Look at the graphic given below and notes for more clarification.

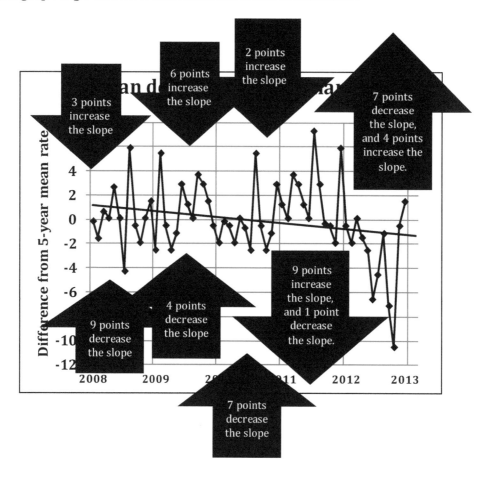

Example 9

The graph represents data on the non-vegetarian foods habits of different age group natives living in a country. The graph shows the percentage of natives preferring vegetarian food, and the percentage of non-vegetarians preferring varieties of non-vegetarian foods across all groups.

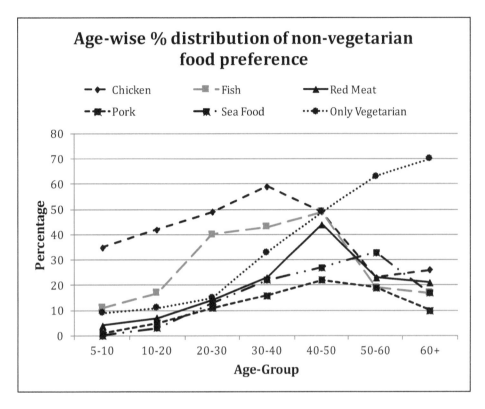

Based on the given information, use the drop-down menus to most accurately complete the following statements:

(A) Approximately _____ % of the natives in the country belonging to 40–50 age group eat red meat.

    (A) 22

    (B) 44

    (C) 50

    (D) 88

(B) The greatest percentage increase in the number of vegetarians calculated from one age group to the subsequent is _____ %. (Assume that the population is same for all age groups.)

    (A) 36

    (B) 48

    (C) 100

    (D) 120

Solution—Part A

In the 40–50 age group, 50% natives prefer vegetarian food, hence the same percentage of natives, i.e., 50% prefer non-vegetarian food. Out of these 50% non-vegetarian natives, ≈ 44% prefer red meat. It means that 50% of 44% = 22% natives prefer red meat.

The correct answer is option A.

Solution—Part B

The percent increase from one age group to the succeeding one is calculated as:

$$\frac{\text{vegetarians in the } n^{\text{th}} \text{ age group} - \text{vegetarians in the } (n-1)^{\text{th}} \text{ age group}}{\text{vegetarians in the } (n-1)^{\text{th}} \text{ age group}} \times 100\%$$

or

$$\frac{(\% \text{ vegetarians in the } n^{\text{th}} \text{ age group} \times \text{population}) - (\% \text{ vegetarians in the } (n-1)^{\text{th}} \text{ age group} \times \text{population})}{\% \text{ vegetarians in the } (n-1)^{\text{th}} \text{ age group} \times \text{population}} \times 100\%$$

Since the population is same for all the age groups, we can rewrite the above as:

$$\frac{\% \text{ vegetarians in the } n^{\text{th}} \text{ age group} - \% \text{ vegetarians in the } (n-1)^{\text{th}} \text{ age group}}{\% \text{ vegetarians in the } (n-1)^{\text{th}} \text{ age group}} \times 100\%$$

It would be time-consuming to calculate the percent increase of vegetarians for all groups, hence not advisable. You can observe the graph to shortlist the probable contenders.

Looking at the formula above, you can infer that to get the greatest value the numerator, or the difference of percentages between two succeeding age groups, should be high, while the denominator, or the percent value for the predecessor age group, should be low.

Based on this analysis, you will find that the answer is the 30–40 age group as the percent jump in the number of vegetarians from the age group 20–30 to 30–40 age group is ≈ 33% − 15% =≈ 18%. This is the highest numerator that any of the groups have. Although the numerator (≈ 18%) of 30–40 age group is equal to that of age group 40–50, denominator of age group 40–50 is ≈ 33%, which is greater than for age group 20–30 (15%). So, the answer would be:

$$\frac{\approx 18}{\% \, 15\%} \times 100\% =\approx 120\%.$$

The correct answer is option D.

If you are curious, here are the values of percent increase for all age groups:

Age Group	5-10	10-20	20-30	30-40	40-50	50-60	60+
% Value for age group	9	11	15	33	50	63	70
% Increase over the previous group ($\times 100\%$)	=	$\frac{11-9}{9}$	$\frac{15-11}{11}$	$\frac{33-15}{15}$	$\frac{50-33}{33}$	$\frac{63-50}{50}$	$\frac{70-63}{63}$
	=	22%	36%	***120%***	51%	29%	11%

Chapter 5

Two-Part Analysis

5.1 Strategies and Concepts

Out of four parts in the IR section—the GI, TA, MSR, and Two-Part—you will find the Two-Part section more familiar than the others. However, you have to answer two parts in each question—as opposed to one part in Quantitative Ability and Verbal Ability questions.

There are three types of questions asked in Two-Part part:

(1) Quants-based

(2) Logic-based

(3) Critical-Reasoning-based

A Two-Part question ask two aspects of a question. The answers to both parts must be compatible with each other.

5.1.1 Two-Part Quants

Two-Part-Quant questions are more focused than one-part GMAT Quant PS/DS questions, which are more trickier and vaster in scope. Two-Part Quant questions have comparatively lengthy word problems that focus on basic arithmetic and preliminary algebra. You must possess good problem-solving skills to solve them.

A word of caution: there are two answers, so be careful to mark each part with its respective answer.

Those who are good at Quants will find Two-Part Quant-based questions relatively easy. The key is to prepare well for Quants.

5.2   Process of Solving Two-Part Quant Questions

(1) *Understand the question*

Solving Two-Part-Quant questions is similar to solving any Quant questions:
Read the information and understand it; translate it into mathematical language, and write it on the scratch board.

(2) *Develop an approach*

There could be two or more ways to approach a question. Many times, solving one part leads to the solution of the other part.

(3) *Apply the approach*

Apply the approach you developed in the previous step. There may be a question where you end up with only one linear equation with two variables. Though here, there is no unique solution possible for the question, but many consistent and compatible solutions are always possible. Only one such consistent and compatible solution would be given in the options.

Your last step is to click correct radio buttons.

5.2.1   Two-Part Logic Games

Two-Part Logic-based questions are like those you might have come across in the LSAT or other aptitude tests. The narration of these questions is comparatively lengthy, and involves a mix of quantitative and verbal skills.

This book contains a couple of good logic-based questions.

The process of solving logic-based questions is similar to that of quant-based questions, except that you have to think twice.

5.2.2   Two-Part Critical Reasoning

Two-Part CR-based questions are like Critical Reasoning questions you come across in the GMAT Verbal section. The questions may test your critical reasoning skills by asking about two aspects of widely known concepts such as assumption, strengthen and weaken, evaluate, strategize, and role play.

In a typical Verbal-CR question, if you are asked to strengthen the argument, you can simply ignore the options that weaken the argument. However, in Two-Part CR-based questions, you will be asked to both strengthen and weaken the argument. Out of 5–6 option choices, 2–3 of them may strengthen the argument, while the other 2–3 options may weaken the argument.

Nevertheless, compared to Verbal-CR questions, Two-Part CR-based questions are relatively easy. There might be only 2–3 options for each aspect, as opposed to Verbal-CR questions, in which all five options may be crafted to test only one aspect.

Those who are good at answering Verbal-CR questions will find the Two-Part CR section relatively easy. The key is to prepare well for the Verbal-CR section.

Let us look at some GMAT-like questions now.

5.3 Examples: Two-Part Quant-based Questions

Example 1

For a right circular cylinder, r stands for the radius of its base, h for its height, A for its curved surface area, and V for its volume. In terms of the variables A and V, select in the table the expressions that represent height h and radius r.

Make only two selections, one in each column.

	A	B	
	r	h	
A	○	○	$\frac{A^2}{4\pi V}$
B	○	○	$\frac{2V}{A}$
C	○	○	$\frac{A^2 V}{8\pi}$
D	○	○	$\frac{2A}{V}$
E	○	○	$\frac{A}{V}$

Solution—Part A

Let us understand the question. This is a variable-based two-part question on solids–cylinders. The question tests your knowledge about relationships between the radius of the base, height, surface area, and volume of a cylinder. You have to select the expressions in the table that represent its height h and radius r only in terms of volume V and curved surface area A.

An approach would be to write down the formulas for the curved surface area and volume of a cylinder, then manipulate them to get r and h in terms of volume V and curved surface area A.

First, shortlist the options to probable ones, or eliminate a few non-probable ones. Here, though, there is no such option that can be easily eliminated. So, follow the next step:

Write down the formulas for curved surface area and volume. The formulas are:

$$\text{Curved surface area, } A = \pi dh = 2\pi rh$$
$$\text{Volume, } V = \frac{\pi d^2 h}{4} = \pi r^2 h$$

Observe the formula for the volume, $V = \pi r^2 h$. If you rewrite it as $V = 2\pi rh \times \frac{r}{2}$, you find that you can replace the term $2\pi rh$ with the curved surface area A of a cylinder. So, replace it with A.

Hence, the relationship becomes $V = \dfrac{Ar}{2} \Rightarrow r = \dfrac{2V}{A}$.

So the answer for the first part is B.

Solution—Part B

As stated in previous question, observe the given options to shortlist probables, or eliminate a few options. However, again in this part, there is no such option that can be easily eliminated. So, follow the next step:

Rewrite the formulas of curved surface area and volume. The formulas are:

$$\text{Curved surface area, } A = 2\pi r h$$

$$\text{Volume, } V = \pi r^2 h$$

Manipulate the formulas to get h only in terms of A and V.

Observe the formula for the curved surface area, $A = 2\pi r h$. If you rewrite it as $r = \dfrac{A}{2}\pi h$, and plug the value of r into the formula for V, then the relationship becomes:

$$V = \pi \times \left(\frac{A^2}{4\pi^2 h^2} \right) \times h$$

After the calculation, it becomes $V = \dfrac{A^2}{4\pi h}$ or $h = \dfrac{A^2}{4\pi V}$.

So the answer for the second part is A.

The correct answers are options B and A.

Example 2

For positive values of n, M is defined such that

$$2M_{n+2} + (M_n)^2 - M_{n+1} = 1.$$

Also given that $M_6 = \dfrac{1}{2}$. Select the values of M_4, and M_5 in the table such that they are jointly compatible with these conditions.

Make only two selections, one in each column.

	A	B	
	M_4	M_5	
A	○	○	-2
B	○	○	$-\sqrt{2}$
C	○	○	1
D	○	○	$\sqrt{2}$
E	○	○	4

Solution—Both Parts

Let us understand the question. The equation given is a quadratic equation with three variables. The value of one variable is given. You have to find the jointly compatible values of the other two variables.

Since the equation is a generic equation, given for any three successive applicable variables, you must approach the question such that you are able to build a relationship among M_4, M_5, and M_6.

Observe the given options to shortlist probable or eliminate a few non-probable options. However, there is no option that can be easily eliminated because the desired equation(s) are not yet established. Once you form the equation(s), you can then eliminate options.

Follow the next step: Establish a relationship only among the variables M_4, M_5, and M_6.

As discussed previously, $2M_{n+2} + (M_n)^2 - M_{n+1} = 1$ is a relationship among three successive terms, so to establish the relationship among M_4, M_5, and M_6, consider $n = 4$.

By plugging in $n = 4$, you get $2M_6 + (M_4)^2 - M_5 = 1$

Again, by plugging in the value of $M_6 = \frac{1}{2}$, you get:

$$2 \left(\tfrac{1}{2} \right) + (M_4)^2 - M_5 = 1$$
$$\Rightarrow (M_4)^2 - M_5 = 0$$
$$\Rightarrow (M_4)^2 = M_5 \quad \text{or} \quad M_4 = \pm\sqrt{M_5}.$$

The above relationship has two variables, so a unique solution is not possible. However, you can still get consistent solutions. The question only asks for a set of compatible values of M_4 and M_5 present in the table.

By hit and trial, you can find a set of compatible values from the table: $M_4 = -2$ and $M_5 = 4$, so the correct answers for both the parts are options A and E respectively. Mark answers in the correct order; marking answers E and A would be wrong.

The correct answers are options A and E.

Point to Remember

Unique Solutions vs. Consistent Solutions

Say you have an equation: $x + 2y = 8$. It has two variables, x and y. If you plug in $x = 2$ in the equation, you get $y = 3$. Is that a solution to the equation? Well, Yes!

Now, if you plug in $x = 4$, you get $y = 2$. Is it a solution to the equation? Well, Yes! Similarly, you can plug any number for a variable and get the corresponding value of the other variable. Both the solutions ($x = 2$, $y = 3$ and $x = 4$, $y = 2$) are consistent solutions to the equation $x + 2y = 8$, however they are NOT unique solutions.

What is a unique solution?

Well, to get the unique solution, if the equation has two variables, then you need two simultaneous equations. In general, if an equation has n variables, you need n independent equations to get a unique solution.

So, suppose you bring in another equation: $2x + y = 7$. Solving both the equations simultaneously, you get $x = 2$ and $y = 3$. That is a **unique solution**, as each variable can have only one value.

Example 3

Suppose you have the following list of executives in a company's departments:

Department 1: Robin, Betty, Yasin, Tom

Department 2: Ponting, Tony, Olga

Department 3: Palvi, George, Brown, Steve, Jack

Department 4: Balki, Whitney, Silvy

The HR department of the company is selecting executives from the above departments to form three new teams consisting of four executives in each team. For each team, no more than two executives can be selected from one department, and executives from no more than three departments can be selected. Each team must have at least a manager-level executive. Betty, Palvy, and Brown are manager-level executives.

The first three executives selected for each of the teams are:

Team 1	Team 2	Team 3
Yasin	Palvy	George
Ponting	Steve	Brown
Silvy	Robin	Tony

Select an executive that could be selected as the fourth executive for all three teams, and select an executive that could not be selected as the fourth executive for any of the teams.

	A	B	
	Can be selected	**Cannot be selected**	
A	○	○	Olga
B	○	○	Jack
C	○	○	Betty
D	○	○	Balky
E	○	○	Tom

Solution—Both Parts

Analyze each option and apply a process of elimination.

  (A) *Olga*: Olga cannot be in Team 1, as it lacks a manager and Olga is not the one. The only executive, Team 1 can have is Betty (a manager). She can also be in Team 2 or 3.

  (B) *Jack*: Jack cannot in be Team 1, as it lacks a manager and Jack is not the one. Neither can be be in Team 2 as Palvy and Steve are already there from his department nor can be be in Team 3, as George and Brown are already there from his department. (There cannot be more than two executives from a department.)

   So, **Jack** is the answer for second part, **"Cannot be selected."**

  (C) *Betty*: We concluded in the option A that Betty must be in Team 1. Betty can also be in either Team 2 or Team 3.

   Betty is the correct answer for the first part, **"Can be selected."**

The correct answers are options C and B.

Example 4

Working individually, Alex, Betty, and Cherry can do a job in 8, 24, and 48 hours, respectively. It was decided that each of them will work on the job successively for an hour. Anyone can start the work and others will follow. Select in the table "Minimum hours" and "Maximum hours" required to complete the job.

Make only two selections, one in each column.

	A	B	
	Minimum hours	**Maximum hours**	
A	○	○	15
B	○	○	15.5
C	○	○	16.17
D	○	○	17
E	○	○	17.33

Solution—Both Parts

You must identify that Alex is the fastest worker, finishing 1/8 of the work in an hour, while Cherry is the slowest worker, finishing 1/48 of the work in an hour.

Also, note that *Anyone can start the work and the others will follow.* It means that anybody: Alex, Betty, or Cherry can start or finish the job.

When Alex, Betty, and Cherry each work, in that order, for an hour, then in a total of three hours, they accomplish:

$$\frac{1}{8} + \frac{1}{24} + \frac{1}{48} = \frac{9}{48} = \left(\frac{3}{16}\right)^{\text{th}} \text{ of the job.}$$

After five rounds, in a total of $5 \times 3 = 15$ hours, they complete $\frac{3}{16} \times 5 = \frac{15}{16}$ of the job. So, $1 - \frac{15}{16} = \frac{1}{16}$ of the job remains.

To find the **maximum time to do the job**, choose the **slowest worker (Cherry)** to take the next turn. She does another $\left(\frac{1}{48}\right)^{\text{th}}$ of the work in an hour. Then choose the next slower worker, Betty, to do another $\left(\frac{1}{24}\right)^{\text{th}}$ of the job in the next hour. This covers the remaining part of the job after the initial five rounds:

$$\frac{1}{48} + \frac{1}{24} = \frac{3}{48} = \frac{1}{16} = \text{remaining job}$$

So, the maximum time to do the job would be $15 + 1 + 1 = 17$ hours. The answer for the second part of the question is option D, 17 hrs.

To find the **minimum time to do the job**, after the initial five rounds, select the **fastest worker, Alex**, to take the next turn. He would need just $\frac{1}{2}$ an hour to do the remaining $\left(\frac{1}{16}\right)^{th}$ of the job.

So, the minimum time to do the job is $15 + 0.5 = 15.5$ hours. The answer for the first part of the question is option B, 15.5 hrs.

The correct answers are options B and D.

5.4 Examples: Two-Part Verbal-based Questions

Example 5

Railway Safety Commissioner: "The Railways Ministry claims that the railways' safety lapses have been caused by my policies and that I am responsible for the lapses. Although I admit that **the railways has suffered a couple of fatal accidents during my tenure**, I do not agree that I am at fault. The safety policies of the previous Railway Safety Commissioner are to blame, and **had it not been for the safety policies of my administration, the current safety system would have been even worse.**"

In the argument above, the two phrases in boldface play specific roles. Select the appropriate Boldface 1 or 2 to be consistent with the role it plays in the argument.

Make two selections, one in each column.

	A	B	
	Boldface 1	**Boldface 2**	
A	○	○	is a consequence of the Railway Ministry's claims.
B	○	○	is the main conclusion
C	○	○	supports the conclusion
D	○	○	is a fact, which the Railway Safety Commissioner believes does not contradict his own conclusion
E	○	○	is evidence of unethical activity on the part of the Railway Safety Commissioner

Solution—Both Parts

Understanding the argument

The Railway Ministry claims that the current Railway Safety Commissioner's safety policy is the reason for security lapses. However, the Railway Safety Commissioner contradicts the claim.

Railway Safety Commissioner's position: "I am not responsible for it (security lapses)."

Although he admits that two major accidents occurred during his tenure, he reasons that his predecessor's policies were to blame and not his. Furthermore, he strengthens his position by stating that had his own policies not been implemented, the situation could have been worse than what it now is.

Conclusion: I (Railway Safety Commissioner) am not at fault for this problem.

Let us dissect the argument and understand the positions of Ministry and the Railway Safety Commissioner:

- *Ministry:* the current Railway Safety Commissioner's policies are at fault.

- *Railway Safety Commissioner:* I am not at fault. I admit that a problem occurred during my tenure, but my predecessor is at fault.

- *Boldface 1:* is a fact because of which the Railway Ministry considers the Railway Safety Commissioner liable.

- *Boldface 2:* is the Railway Safety Commissioner's opinion, with which he strengthens his position and supports the conclusion.

Answer Choice Explanation:

Of the given options, the Boldface 1 phrase is an admission of a fact that the Railway Safety Commissioner believes does not contradict his conclusion, while Boldface 2 supports his conclusion of "I am not at fault".

The correct answers are options D and C.

Example 6

Consultant: The decline in market share of the Whito 3-kg detergent pack is a matter of concern. There could be many predictive reasons. The competing brand, EcoWash, is always on the lookout to gain Whito's substantial market share. Also, due to adverse judgments in consumer courts against WhiteMagic detergent—the brand that kept EcoWash's detergent sales in check—WhiteMagic's sales are suffering, providing an opportunity for EcoWash. Usually, customers prefer the detergent from the brand that already has an established soap cake selling in the market.

Indicate in the table which cause-and-effect sequence would most likely, according to the consultant, result in a decline of market share of Whito detergent.

Make two selections, one in each column.

	A	B	
	Cause	**Effect**	
A	○	○	An increase in the market share of EcoWash soap cake
B	○	○	An increase in the market share of EcoWash detergent
C	○	○	An increase in the market share of WhiteMagic detergent
D	○	○	A decrease in the market share of EcoWash soap cake
E	○	○	A decrease in the market share of EcoWash detergent

Solution—Both Parts

Understanding the argument

You are asked to provide a cause-and-effect sequence that would, according to the consultant, result in a decline of market share of the Whito 3-kg detergent pack. The question suggests that the answers are dependent on each other, so the correct answer of part A will depend on the correct answer of part B, and vice versa. The passage states that one factor contributing to decline of market share of the Whito 3-kg detergent pack is the success of the detergent made by a competing brand named EcoWash.

EcoWash brand's detergent eats up the market share of Whito brand, and so a causal sequence that has as its effect—an increase in market share of EcoWash detergent may produce a decline in the market share of Whito 3-kg's detergent. This suggests that option B may be the correct response for part B of the question. However, this depends on whether one of the other statements in the table describes a cause suggested by the consultant.

The last sentence of the argument implies that if a detergent brand does well in the market, its cake variant also does well. This also applies to the EcoWash brand. The consultant may have taken an increase in the market share of EcoWash soap cake as the *cause* (Part A, option A) to produce the *effect* (Part B, option B) of increase in the market share of EcoWash detergent, thereby causing a decline in Whito's sales (the conclusion).

The correct answers are option A and B.

Example 7

ABC Farms has two farms in the city: one in Somanaphate, and the other in Valsad. The situation at both the farms were alike in all aspects, including the amount of exposure to sunlight, the amount of water, the quality of the seeds, and the degree of manure use—except for the degree of fertilizing of soil with biochar. The degree of fertilization was twice as much for the Valsad farm as for the Somanaphate farm. The final crop yield from both farms was approximately the same. ABC Farms claims that fertilizing the soil with biochar was ineffective.

In the table, select the changes that the farmer could make in the Somanaphate and Valsad farms, respectively, that together would be most helpful in testing ABC Farms claim.

Make only two selections, one in each column.

	A	B	
	Somanaphate	Valsad	
A	○	○	Double the quantity of the manure
B	○	○	Test the quality of the seeds
C	○	○	Change the brand of biochar
D	○	○	Do away with biochar altogether
E	○	○	Exercise weed control

Solution—Both Parts

First understand the argument and its conclusion.

Claim: Fertilizing the soil with biochar is ineffective.

This asserts that fertilizing the soil with biochar does not affect crop yield. You have to evaluate whether this claim made by the farmer is correct.

Answer Choice Explanation

(A) Option A is out of scope. Doubling the quantity of the manure will not help. The effectiveness of the manure is not called in question.

(B) The argument states that quality of seeds was same for both the farms; hence testing the quality of seeds is of no significance.

(C) Changing the brand of biochar will not help explain why the biochar was not effective, as the farmer's assertion is that biochar itself is ineffective, not just a specific brand.

(D) Option D is the correct answer for both parts: do away with biochar in both the farms. By not amending the soils with biochar, the farmer can evaluate his assumption by measuring the yields of both the farms while keeping other parameters the same. If the difference in yield is insignificant, his claim is right; otherwise it is wrong.

(E) Exercising weed control is out of scope.

The correct answers are option D and D.

Chapter 6

Multi-Source Reasoning

6.1 Strategies and Concepts

Out of four parts of the IR-GI, TA, MSR, and Two-Part sections, the MSR section may look more scary, but in reality, it is not so. The MSR format is more along the lines of Reading Comprehension format. Unlike dataset of TA, Two-Part, and GI sections, an MSR dataset may have 3–5 questions. You will find that one MSR dataset in *Official Guide online companion* has as many as six questions. However, during an exam, you will usually come across only three questions.

As stated earlier, that there are 2–3 tabs of information in an MSR dataset, but you can only see one tab at a time. This will not be a great challenge if you have sifted through spreadsheets in Excel, in which you view only one sheet at a time. You can view 2–3 tabs with a click of mouse. As with the TA section, the MSR part has interactive prompts.

There are three types of questions asked in the MSR section:

(1) Quants-based

(2) Verbal-based

(3) A mix of Quants and Verbal-based

6.2   Process of Solving MSR Questions

(1) *Understand the data set*

Read the information given in each tab. Understand it, but do not read it more than once at this stage. Then read the question. Remember that only one question will be visible at a time. Keep in mind that you have on average 7.5 minutes to answer all three MSR questions.

(2) *Understand the question*

Read the question and make sure you understand it, so you know what you are looking for. Read the tabs again to gather information for the answer.

Repeat this for other two questions. By the time you answer the third question, you should have read the tabs at least three times.

(3) *Develop an approach to solve the question*

You will have to gather information from more than one tab. Say, for example, a question asks about a company's profit. Suppose Tab 1 gives details about revenue and sales, whereas Tab 2 gives details about budget and cost. You must sift through both tabs to get the answer.

(4) *Apply the approach*

Apply the previous step to finally solve the problem. Do your scratch work neatly, as you may need to use some calculations again to answer another question.

6.3 Examples

Examples 1–3

Tab 1

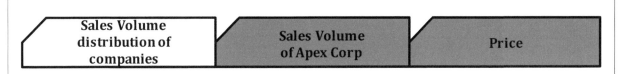

In the mosquito-repellent product category, there are five major companies in the retail business. The pie chart represents company-wide sales volume distribution of mosquito-repellent products.

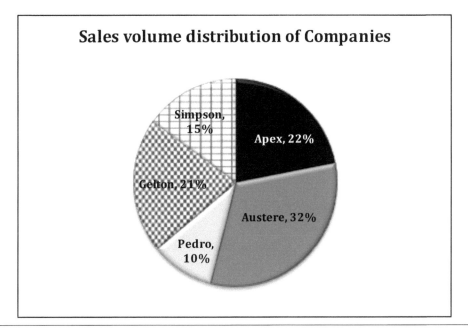

Tab 2

Sales Volume distribution of companies	Sales Volume of Apex Corp	Price

The table below presents the region-wise and product-wise sales volume distribution of the Apex Corporation.

Products	North	South	East	West	Total
Mosquito Repellent Coil	124	140	106	50	420
Mosquito Repellent Refill	100	110	90	70	370
Mosquito Repellent Cream	46	140	98	6	290
Mosquito Repellent Gel	24	98	32	16	170
Total	**294**	**488**	**326**	**142**	**1250**

Unit: '000 cartons

Tab 3

| Sales Volume distribution of companies | Sales Volume of Apex Corp | Price |

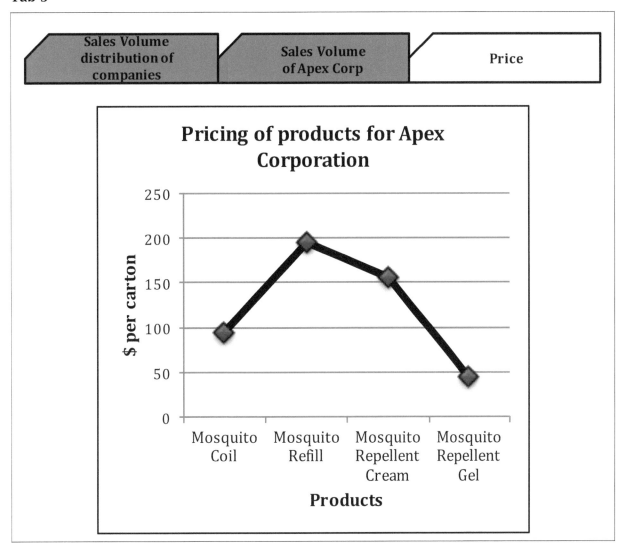

Pricing of products for Apex Corporation

Question 1

For each of the following statements, select "Yes" if the statement is true based on the information provided; otherwise select "No".

	Yes	No	
A	○	○	The difference between the sales volume of Austere Corporation and Pedro Corporation is more than 1,250,000 cartons.
B	○	○	For the Apex Corporation, sales revenue from the Eastern region is more than that from the Northern region.
C	○	○	For the Apex Corporation, sales revenue from Mosquito Coil is more than that from Mosquito Refill.

Solution

- *Part A:* From Tab 1, you know that the percent sales volume for the Apex Corporation is 22% of the total sales volume of all five companies. From Tab 2, you know that the sales volume of the Apex Corporation is 1,250,000 cartons. So, 22% × (total sales) = $1,250,000$.

  Again, from Tab 1, you will find that the percent difference of the sales volume of the Austere Corporation and the Pedro Corporation is $32 - 10 = 22\%$, which is equal to the percent sales volume of Apex. Hence, the answer is exactly 1,250,000, not more.

  The correct answer is "No".

- *Part B:* In a nutshell, you are asked to find out whether

  Revenue from the Eastern region > Revenue from the Northern region

  This question may appear to be time-consuming, but the GMAT never asks a question that is too time-consuming. So, there must be an alternate approach.

  We find that the sales volumes of the Coil and Refill are more for the Northern region than for the Eastern region, while the opposite is true for the Cream and Gel. You must analyze which mosquito repellent(s) will contribute more in revenue to a region when sales volumes are multiplied with their respective prices. Clearly, the impact of the Cream type is very high, as the Eastern region sells $98,000 - 46,000 = 52,000$ more mosquito repellent Cream than does the Northern region. Also, its price ($150 per carton) is second highest among all the products. This is going to contribute more in revenue to the Eastern region compared to the Northern region. Though Northern region sells $100,000 - 90,000 = 10,000$ more units of the highest priced ($195 per carton) mosquito repellent Refill, its impact is relatively low as $10,000 \ll 52,000$. Similarly, though Northern region sells $124,000 - 106,000 = 18,000$ more units of the low priced ($95 per carton) mosquito repellent Coil, its impact is relatively low. So collectively, we find that $(10,000 + 24,000 = 34,000) \ll 52,000$. So, the answer would be "Yes." In fact, the Eastern-region revenue is more than Northern-region's by $4,760,000.

The correct answer is "Yes".

The table below presents the computation.

Products & Price	North	East
Mosquito Repellent Coil ($95)	$124 \times 95 = 11780$	$106 \times 95 = 10070$
Mosquito Repellent Refill ($195)	$100 \times 195 = 19500$	$90 \times 195 = 17550$
Mosquito Repellent Cream ($155)	$46 \times 155 = 7130$	$98 \times 155 = 15190$
Mosquito Repellent Gel ($45)	$24 \times 45 = 1080$	$32 \times 45 = 1440$
Total ($'000)	39490	44250

- *Part C:* Fetching the data from Tabs 2 and 3, you will find that the carton price of the Refill ($195 per carton) is almost double that of the Coil ($95 per carton), while sales volume of the Refill is a mere $\approx 10\%$ less than that of the Coil. Collectively, the revenue from the Refill sales would be more than that from the Coil sales.

The correct answer is "No".

Question 2

If the Pedro Corporation sells exactly the same kinds of mosquito repellent products as does Apex Corporation: Coils, Refills, Cream, and Gel, and it has the same proportion of sales volume for the four products as does Apex Corporation, then how many Gel cartons did the Pedro Corporation sell?

(A) 38,000

(B) 77,000

(C) 170,000

(D) 374,000

(E) 1250,000

Solution

The sales volume of Gel for the Apex Corporation is 170,000. The percent share of sales volume for the Apex Corporation is 22% of all five companies, while for Pedro, it is 10%. Clearly, the sales volume of Gel for Pedro was

$$170,000 \times \frac{10\%}{22\%} = 77,000 \text{ cartons}$$

The correct answer is option B.

Question 3

Keeping the total sales volume the same for the Apex Corporation, which of the following rearrangement of sales volume of products will generate more sales revenue than currently?

- **(A)** Reduce the Mosquito Coil sales volume by half and increase the sales volume of Mosquito Repellent Gel by the same amount.

- **(B)** Reduce the Mosquito Refill sales volume by one-third and increase the sales volume of Mosquito Repellent Cream by the same amount.

- **(C)** Reduce the Mosquito Cream sales volume by 20% and increase the sales volume of Mosquito Repellent Gel by the same amount.

- **(D)** Reduce the Mosquito Coil sales volume by 33.33% and increase the sales volume of Mosquito Repellent Cream by the same amount.

- **(E)** Reduce the Mosquito Repellent Cream sales volume by 66.66% and increase the sales volume of Mosquito Coil by the same amount.

Solution

In all the options, the sales volume of one kind of mosquito repellent is reduced and that of another kind is increased by the same amount. So, the revenue can be increased if a product with a lower price is replaced by a product with a higher price. In one instance, reduced sales volume of the Coil ($95 per carton) is offset by the relatively high-priced Mosquito Cream ($155 per carton). This move will certainly increase the revenue. For the other options, the revenue will decrease.

The correct answer is option D.

Examples 4–6

Tab 1

| Mike, Chief economist, on BRICS countries | Professor Walter on BRICS countries |

The notion that the era of emerging BRICS countries is over—and that among them only China would make it to the group of high-income countries—is outlandish. No doubt the growth rates in the BRICS group of Brazil, Russia, India, China, and South Africa have been affected by the global slowdown, and countries such as India have been further singed by capital-flow reversals. However, this is a temporary phenomenon that will peter out sooner rather than later. The BRICS countries' economies are bound to reinvent the global economic order—and even fashion it in their own image—once the macroeconomic balances are restored and foreign investment flows rebound, boosted by reforms.

Similarly, the argument that the rest of the BRICS countries will fall by the wayside while China continues to march ahead is flawed. China's growth rate is almost half that of peak levels. It's also facing a double whammy: 1) its export-led economy has been badly hit by the slowdown in advanced country markets, and 2) rising wages and a shortage of skills erode its competitive base, as it struggles to shift over to a domestic consumption-based growth model. This will probably help other BRICS countries, such as India, make new inroads into the global markets for manufactured goods, and thus close in fast on China.

In fact, the most recent trends on the global Greenfield investments, which exclude mergers and acquisitions, validate this argument. The numbers show that while the new FDI (Foreign Direct Investment) projects in China have almost halved after the global slowdown, the other BRICS countries haven't been so badly bruised. On the contrary, the gap between China and other BRICS countries has in fact shrunk, with India accounting for 30% of the Greenfield FDI projects, as compared to China's 40% share.

Tab 2

| Mike, Chief economist, on BRICS countries | Professor Walter on BRICS countries |

The economist Mike's assessment that the BRICS era is at an end is right on the money. Despite witnessing robust economic growth in the last decade, each of the BRICS countries faces a unique set of problems today. The recent global economic downturn has exposed structural infirmities that will prevent these economies from returning to a high-growth trajectory anytime soon. Besides, it is not realistic to expect these emerging markets to grow faster from a higher GDP base rather than from their previous low threshold.

In India, the economy is wracked by a Rupee in free-fall, high inflation, and a burgeoning current account deficit. Recent months have seen significant capital outflows, with foreign investors opting to park their funds in a recovering U.S. economy. The petering-out of growth sentiments is directly related to the political leadership's failure to affect a much-needed second wave of economic reforms. Furthermore, with policy paralysis expected to continue, the India-growth story remains in limbo. In both Brazil and Russia, the weakening of commodity prices has hit the economies hard, exposing their over-reliance on natural resources as cash cows. Meanwhile, South Africa's economy has been hurting since a recession that affected several crucial industries. In China, the economy is transitioning from resource-intensive, investment-led growth to a consumption-oriented pattern. Add to this the massive global pressure to appreciate the Yuan, and it is clear that China would need to affect a not-so-easy overhaul of its economic model to maintain high growth. However, as the economist Mike pointed, given China's planned economic model and ability to move resources without political missteps, it is best placed from among the BRICS nations to pull out of the middle-income trap. Taken together, the global heft that the BRICS bloc wielded is over. While these emerging markets will continue to grow, they will need to get used to moderate rates of growth.

Question 4

For each of the following issues, select "Agree" if, based on the information provided, it can be inferred that both the commentators would hold similar positions on the issue. Otherwise, select "Disagree".

	Agree	Disagree	
A	○	○	Acknowledging that the BRICS countries had experienced good economic growth in the past
B	○	○	The timeframe in which the BRICS countries will bounce back to good economic growth
C	○	○	China's ability to transform into a consumption-oriented economy soon

Solution

- *Part A:*

  In Tab 1, the second sentence (paragraph 1), (Mike) says, "*No doubt the growth rates in the BRICS group of Brazil, Russia, India, China, and South Africa have been affected by the global slowdown...*" The fourth sentence (paragraph 1), says, "*The BRICS countries' economies are bound to reinvent the global economic order—and even fashion it in their own image...*"

  Look at Tab 2, the second sentence (paragraph 1), Professor Walter says "*Despite witnessing robust economic growth in the last decade, each of the BRICS countries faces a unique set of problems today.*"

  Both would agree on experiencing good economic growth in the past.

- *Part B:*

  In Tab 1, the third sentence in the first paragraph says, "*However, this is a temporary phenomenon that will peter out sooner rather than later.*" So, Mike opines that the BRICS economies will bounce back soon.

  In Tab 2, the first paragraph, third sentence, says, "*The recent global economic downturn has exposed structural infirmities that will **prevent these economies from returning to a high-growth trajectory anytime soon.***" So, Professor Walter opines that the BRICS economies will not be able to bounce back soon.

  Both would disagree on the recovery timeframe.

- *Part C:*

  In Tab 1, the second sentence in the second paragraph says, " *its [China's] competitive base, as it struggles to shift over to a **domestic consumption-based growth model**.*" So, Mike opines that it will be difficult for China to shift over to a consumption-based economy.

In Tab 2, the sixth sentence in the second paragraph says, "*In China, the economy is* **transitioning** *from resource-intensive, investment-led growth to a consumption-oriented pattern.*" So, Professor Walter opines that Chinese economy on the course transforming to consumption-oriented economy.

Both would disagree on this issue.

Question 5

For each of the following issues, select "India" if, based on the information provided, it can be inferred that the issue pertains to India; otherwise, select "China".

	India	China	
A	◯	◯	The degree of political impediment in the country to economic growth
B	◯	◯	The severity of impact on the country due to withdrawal of new FDI projects
C	◯	◯	The global slowdown, along with capital-flow reversal

Solution

- *Part A:*

  Refer to Tab 2, the fifth sentence in the second paragraph, which says, "*Furthermore, with* **policy paralysis** *expected to continue, the India growth story remains in limbo.*" Professor Walter clearly expresses concern over the economic recovery in India due to "policy paralysis," which implies political impediments.

  To confirm that China doesn't have political impediments, again refer to Tab 2, the eighth sentence in the second paragraph, which says, "*However, as the economist points out, given China's planned economic model and ability to move resources without political missteps, . . .*"

  "India" is the correct answer for option A.

- *Part B:*

  Refer to Tab 1, the second sentence of the third paragraph, which says, "*The numbers show that while the* **new FDI (Foreign Direct Investment) projects in China have almost halved after the global slowdown***, the* **other BRICS countries haven't been so badly bruised.***"* Mike clearly expresses that, due to withdrawal of new FDI projects, China is "bruised badly"—meaning impacted severely.

  "China" is the correct answer for option B.

- *Part C:*

  Refer to Tab 1, the second sentence in the first paragraph, which says, "*No doubt the growth rates in the BRICS group of Brazil, Russia, India, China, and South Africa have been affected by the global slowdown, and countries such as India have been further singed by capital-flow reversals.*"

  Refer to Tab 2, the second sentence of the second paragraph, which says, "*Recent months have seen significant capital outflows, with foreign investors opting to park their funds in a recovering U.S. economy.*"

  It can be inferred from both that India has been impacted by global slowdown, along with capital flow reversal.

  "India" is the correct answer for option C.

Question 6

Which of the following *cannot* be inferred based on the information provided?

- **(A)** Brazil's and Russia's economies are dependent on natural resources.

- **(B)** The U.S. economy is benefitting in some way from current economic problems in one of the BRICS countries.

- **(C)** Weakening of commodity prices in Brazil and Russia benefitted China.

- **(D)** Export-led economy is affected by slowdown in advance country markets.

- **(E)** Russia, Brazil, and South Africa each account for much less than 40% of Greenfield FDI projects in BRICS.

Solution

Refer to Tab 2, the fifth sentence in the second paragraph, which says, "*In both Brazil and Russia, the **weakening of commodity prices has hit the economies hard, exposing their over-reliance on natural resources** as cash cows.*" From this, you can infer that Brazil's and Russia's economies are dependent on natural resources (option A). However, regarding the weakening of commodity prices, you can only infer that it has impacted Brazil and Russia hard, not that it has benefitted China.

Option B can also be inferred. Refer to Tab 2, the first sentence of the second paragraph, which says, "*Recent months have seen significant capital outflows, with foreign investors **opting to park their funds in a recovering** U.S. economy.*"

Option D can also be inferred. Refer to Tab 1, the second and third sentences of the second paragraph, which say, "*China's growth rate is almost half that of peak levels. It's also facing a double whammy with its **export-led economy has been badly hit by the slowdown in advanced country markets**, . . .*"

Option E can also be inferred. Refer to Tab 1, the last sentence of the third paragraph, which says, "*On the contrary, the gap between China and other BRICS countries has in fact shrunk, with India accounting for 30% of the Greenfield FDI projects, as compared to China's 40% share.*"

Among the BRICS countries, only India is closest to China, with 30% of the Greenfield FDI projects in BRICS. That means the other BRICS countries must account for much less than 40% of the Greenfield FDI projects in BRICS.

All options can be inferred except option C.

The correct answer is option C.

Chapter 7

Practice Questions

7.1   Table Analysis

1. The table presents the average maximum score, average minimum score, and the Intelligence Quotient (IQ) for Grade X and XII students of City International School for six months.

Months	Grade	Average maximum Score	Average minimum Score	Intelligence Quotient
August	X	66	58	116
August	XII	68	55	120
December	XII	70	49	114
December	X	71	52	117
July	X	71	55	115
July	XII	72	45	116
November	XII	69	51	118
November	X	81	62	119
October	XII	69	45	120
October	X	68	54	121
September	XII	75	56	114
September	X	72	52	121

For each of the following statements, select "Yes" if the statement is true based on the information provided; otherwise, select "No".

	Yes	No	
A	○	○	Compared to grade XII students, grade X students are more consistent with regards to the Intelligence Quotients attribute, taking range as a parameter to measure the consistency.
B	○	○	For any of the given months, the greatest deviation between the average maximum score and average minimum score for grade XII students is more than that for grade X students.
C	○	○	The mean average minimum score for August is more than that for July and for December.

The table sorted by column 2 and by column 5 are given below:

Sorted by column 2

Col 1	Col 2	Col 3	Col 4	Col 5
Months	Grade	Average maximum Score	Average minimum Score	Intelligence Quotient
July	X	71	55	115
August	X	66	58	116
September	X	72	52	121
October	X	68	54	121
November	X	81	62	119
December	X	71	52	117
July	XII	72	45	116
August	XII	68	55	120
September	XII	75	56	114
October	XII	69	45	120
November	XII	69	51	118
December	XII	70	49	114

Sorted by column 5

Col 1	Col 2	Col 3	Col 4	Col 5
Months	Grade	Average maximum Score	Average minimum Score	Intelligence Quotient
September	XII	75	56	114
December	XII	70	49	114
July	X	71	55	115
August	X	66	58	116
July	XII	72	45	116
December	X	71	52	117
November	XII	69	51	118
November	X	81	62	119
August	XII	68	55	120
October	XII	69	45	120
September	X	72	52	121
October	X	68	54	121

Solve yourself:

2. Twelve students from a school secured marks in four subjects. They were scored on Math and Science (out of a possible 100 points), Crafts (out of a possible 25 points), and English (out of a possible 50 points). The table below shows the data.

Students	Math (100)	Craft (25)	English (50)	Science (100)
Angelo	84	9	35	35
Elad	74	5	49	84
Garrison	59	15	37	33
Jack	69	7	41	27
Joe	64	16	31	31
Justin	12	18	5	35
Kevin	89	20	39	37
Lucy	79	7	33	29
Marie	10	20	6	45
Matt	54	22	45	39
Mehul	94	13	43	41
Sean	8	22	50	47

For each of the following statements, select "Yes" if the statement is true based on the information provided; otherwise select "No".

	Yes	No	
A	○	○	The mean score for Math is greater than its median score.
B	○	○	The Math and Science scores for Justine were swapped by mistake. Correcting the mistake will impact neither the median score for Math nor that for Science.
C	○	○	If two new students Suzi and McDonald are included, whose Science scores are 10 and 45, respectively, the median score for Science will increase by 2 points over its current value.

The tables sorted by column 2 and by column 5 are given below:

Sorted by column 2

Col 1	Col 2	Col 3	Col 4	Col 5
Students	Math (100)	Craft (25)	English (50)	Science (100)
Sean	8	22	50	47
Marrie	10	20	6	45
Justin	12	18	5	35
Matt	54	22	45	39
Garysson	59	15	37	33
Joe	64	16	31	31
Jack	69	7	41	27
Elad	74	5	49	84
Lucy	79	7	33	29
Angelo	84	9	35	35
Kevin	89	20	39	37
Mehul	94	13	43	41

Sorted by column 5

Col 1	Col 2	Col 3	Col 4	Col 5
Students	Math (100)	Craft (25)	English (50)	Science (100)
Jack	69	7	41	27
Lucy	79	7	33	29
Joe	64	16	31	31
Garysson	59	15	37	33
Justin	12	18	5	35
Angelo	84	9	35	35
Kevin	89	20	39	37
Matt	54	22	45	39
Mehul	94	13	43	41
Marrie	10	20	6	45
Sean	8	22	50	47
Elad	74	5	49	84

Solve yourself:

3. The table below shows the sales performance of few cars sold by a few car dealerships. It provides information on maximum car sales per month, minimum car sales per month, and the car showroom manager's comments on the month's car sales.

Cars	Company	Maximum sales per month	Minimum sales per month	Manager's comments on sales
3 Series	BMW	10	1	Average
370Z	Nissan	19	11	High
5 Series	BMW	11	2	Average
7 Series	BMW	9	3	Average
Cruze	General Motors	21	12	High
Cube	Nissan	26	20	High
Dayz	Nissan	23	16	High
Expedition	Ford Motors	10	5	Average
Fiesta	Ford Motors	7	2	Low
Grandeur	Hyundai	21	10	High
JM	Hyundai	21	15	High
Juke	Nissan	25	18	High
M Model	BMW	6	0	Low
Maliba	General Motors	10	6	Average
Micra	Nissan	16	8	High
Mini Seven	BMW	8	4	Below average
Moco	Nissan	20	11	High
Mondeo	Ford Motors	21	10	High
Serena	Nissan	21	11	Average
Sonata	Hyundai	20	13	High
Sonic	General Motors	22	16	High
Sunny	Nissan	11	6	Average
Trajet	Hyundai	27	19	High
X5	BMW	22	12	High

For each of the following statements, select "Yes" if the statement is true based on the information provided; otherwise, select "No".

	Yes	No	
A	○	○	At least two cars reporting High sales had their minimum sales per month less than the highest minimum sales per month for a car among those cars that did not report High sales.
B	○	○	The maximum sales per month and minimum sales per month are negatively correlated.
C	○	○	The mean (average) maximum sale per month for Hyundai cars is more than that for BMW cars.

The tables sorted by column 2, column 3, and column 5 are given below:

Sorted by column 2

Col 2	Col 3
Company	Maximum sales per month
BMW	6
BMW	8
BMW	9
BMW	10
BMW	11
BMW	22
Ford Motors	7
Ford Motors	10
Ford Motors	21
General Motors	10
General Motors	21
General Motors	22
Hyundai	20
Hyundai	21
Hyundai	21
Hyundai	27
Nissan	11
Nissan	16
Nissan	19
Nissan	20
Nissan	21
Nissan	23
Nissan	25
Nissan	26

Sorted by column 3

Col 3	Col 4
Maximum sales per month	Minimum sales per month
6	0
7	2
8	4
9	3
10	1
10	5
10	6
11	2
11	6
16	8
19	11
20	11
20	13
21	11
21	12
21	10
21	15
21	10
22	16
22	12
23	16
25	18
26	20
27	19

Sorted by column 5

Col 4	Col 5
Minimum sales per month	Manager's comments on sales
3	Average
1	Average
5	Average
6	Average
2	Average
6	Average
11	Average
4	Below average
8	High
11	High
11	High
13	High
12	High
10	High
15	High
10	High
16	High
12	High
16	High
18	High
20	High
19	High
0	Low
2	Low

Solve yourself:

4. The table shows statistics for a few T20 Cricket teams that played matches throughout the year. A player can play for more than one teams. The result of any match is either a win or a loss.

Teams	Home Ground	Country	Most Valuable Player	Number of matches played	Average score per match	% of matches won
Chennai Super Kings	Chennai	India	Dhoni, Nannes	85	144	46
Deccan Chargers	Hyderabad	India	Kumara	77	128	46
Delhi Daredevils	Delhi	India	Mahela, Sehwag	81	145	54
Kolkata Knight Riders	Kolkata	India	Gambhir	80	154	81
Mumbai Indians	Mumbai	India	Sachin, Malinga	83	165	83
Nagenahira Nagas	Eastern Province	Sri Lanka	Clarke, Kumara	14	144	43
New South Wales Blues	Sydney	Australia	Kumara	24	124	83
Punjab Kings XI	Mohali	India	Clarke	74	125	42
Royal Challengers	Bangalore	India	Gayle	74	121	45
Ruhuna Royals	Southern Province	Sri Lanka	Malinga, Gayle	15	153	47
Southern Redbacks	Adelaide	Australia	Mahela	22	121	87
Tasmanian Tigers	Hobart	Australia	Clarke, Gayle	21	154	43
Uthura Rudra	Dambula	Sri Lanka	Gambhir, Nannes	11	152	46
Uva Next	Badulla	Sri Lanka	Sachin, Mahela	12	154	91
Victorian Bushrangers	Melbourne	Australia	Sachin	26	155	46

For each of the following statements, select "Yes" if the statement is true based on the information provided; otherwise select "No".

	Yes	No	
A	○	○	The teams that included Sachin have the higher average scores per match than the teams that do not have him.
B	○	○	It is likely that the teams that included Clarke did not win a tournament.
C	○	○	The mean average score for Australian teams is more than that for Sri Lankan teams.

The tables sorted by column 3 and by column 6 are given below:

Sorted by column 6

Col 4	Col 5	Col 6
Most Valuable Player	Number of matches played	Average score per match
Mahela	22	121
Gayle	74	121
Kumara	24	124
Clarke	74	125
Kumara	77	128
Dhoni, Nannes	85	144
Clarke, Kumara	14	144
Mahela, Sehwag	81	145
Gambhir, Nannes	11	152
Malinga, Gayle	15	153
Clarke, Gayle	21	154
Gambhir	80	154
Sachin, Mahela	12	154
Sachin	26	155
Sachin, Malinga	83	165

Sorted by column 3

Col 3	Col 4	Col 5	Col 6	Col 7
Country	Most Valuable Player	Number of matches played	Average score per match	% of matches won
Australia	Mahela	22	121	87
Australia	Kumara	24	124	83
Australia	Clarke, Gayle	21	154	43
Australia	Sachin	26	155	46
India	Gayle	74	121	45
India	Clarke	74	125	42
India	Kumara	77	128	46
India	Dhoni, Nannes	85	144	46
India	Mahela, Sehwag	81	145	54
India	Gambhir	80	154	81
India	Sachin, Malinga	83	165	83
Sri Lanka	Clarke, Kumara	14	144	43
Sri Lanka	Gambhir, Nannes	11	152	43
Sri Lanka	Malinga, Gayle	15	153	47
Sri Lanka	Sachin, Mahela	12	154	91

Solve yourself:

7.2 Graphics Interpretation

1. The clustered column chart represents commuters' preferences for buses, trains, and taxis, during a five-year period.

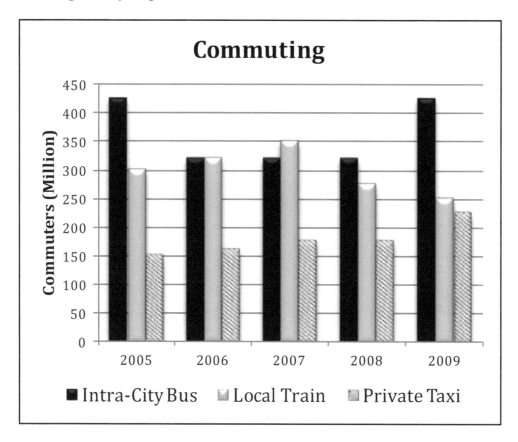

Based on the given information, use the drop-down menus to most accurately complete the following statements.

*   *Part A:*

    In the year 2006, the average bus fare per commuter was $0.75 and that for taxi was $30. The ratio of total revenue from taxi commuters to total revenue from bus commuters in the year 2006 was _____.

    (A)   10 : 1
    (B)   20 : 1
    (C)   30 : 1
    (D)   80 : 1

    Solve yourself:

- *Part B:*

  The number of taxi commuters in the year 2010 would be approximately _____ million, if the number of taxi commuters from the year 2009 to the year 2010 grows at the same rate as from the year 2008 to the year 2009.

  (A) 174
  (B) 224
  (C) 264
  (D) 289

  Solve yourself:

2. The Pie diagram represents the percentage distribution of undergraduate degrees earned by current Post-Graduate B-School students in a select few faculties.

Undergraduate degree distribution

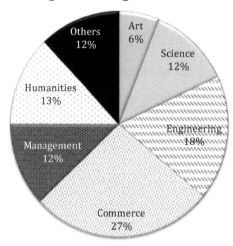

Based on the given information, use the drop-down menus to most accurately complete the following statements.

- *Part A:*

   If 126 students earned their undergraduate degrees from the Art stream, then the number of students who earned their undergraduate degrees from the Engineering stream exceeds that from the Management stream by _____.

   (A) 126
   (B) 252
   (C) 378
   (D) 504
   (E) 2100

   Solve yourself:

- *Part B:*

  The number of undergraduate students from the Engineering stream is more than that from the Science stream by _____.

  (A) 6%

  (B) 33.33%

  (C) 50%

  Solve yourself:

3. The cluster-column chart shows percentage distribution of household owners for seven electronic goods, for the year 2009 and 2012.

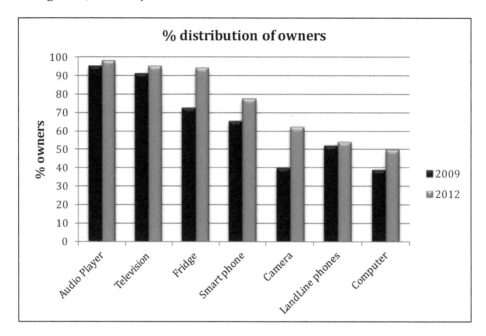

Based on the given information, use the drop-down menus to most accurately complete the following statements.

- *Part A:*

  During the three-year period, the maximum percentage increase in popularity registered by an electronic goods equals _____ %. (Assume that the population of household owners was the same for both the years).

  (A) 3
  (B) 22
  (C) 31
  (D) 55

  Solve yourself:

- *Part B:*

  If the number of owners increased from 606 million in the year 2009 to 1210 million in the year 2012, then the number of new fridges purchased between 2009 and 2012 is _____ million. (Assume that no household owner has sold/discarded a fridge during the period.)

  (A) 22
  (B) 160.7
  (C) 266

(D) 713

Solve yourself:

4. The graph represents the ratios of currencies: Rupees-to-Dollar, Brazilian-Real-to-Dollar, and Dollar-to-Kuwaiti-Dinar, for the period of five months. Rupees-to-Dollar is represented by the primary vertical axis, while Real-to-Dollar and Dollar-to-Dinar are represented by the secondary vertical axis.

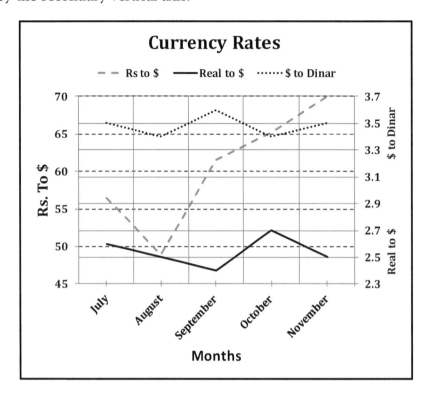

Based on the given information, use the drop-down menus to most accurately complete the following statements.

- *Part A:*

  On July 1, Rupee 5500 amounts to Dinar _____.

  (A) 27.81
  (B) 35
  (C) 337.7
  (D) 350
  (E) 1571

  Solve yourself:

- *Part B:*

  A Mac computer costs Real 2400 on September 1. A man has $1100, Dinar 250, and Rupees 50,000. He would be able to buy a Mac using _____ currency(ies). (Assume that he can use only one type of currency for the whole transaction.)

  (A) Dollar

  (B) Dollar and Rupee

  (C) Rupee and Dinar

  (D) Dinar

  (E) Dinar and Dollar

  Solve yourself:

5. In a school, students major only in Management, Engineering, and Humanities. The Humanities students play only one of the four sports: Soccer, Basketball, Hockey, and Tennis. The Soccer-playing students are Brazilian, Mexican, and Argentinian nationals. The graph shows the percentage distribution of students for majors, the Humanities students' sport preferences, and the nationalities of Soccer playing Humanities students.

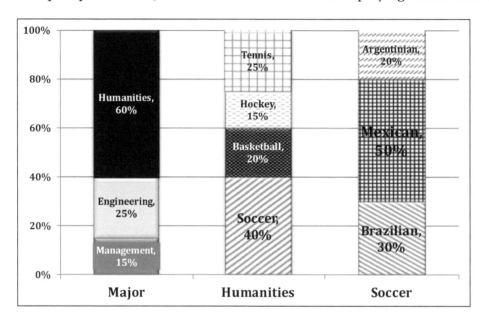

Based on the given information, use the drop-down menus to most accurately complete the following statements.

- *Part A:*

  The humanities students who play tennis are _____ of the total students in the school.

  (A) 7.50%
  (B) 15%
  (C) 25%
  (D) 60%

  Solve yourself:

- *Part B:*

  If there are 80 Mexican Humanities students in the school who play soccer, then the number of students studying Management is _____.

  (A) 50
  (B) 100
  (C) 160
  (D) 400

  Solve yourself:

7.3 2-Part Analysis

Practice Questions (Quants)

1. The average speed of a car was 72 miles/hr for a long journey of d miles. The cost of the fuel was \$3.60/gallon. The average consumption of the fuel was c gallons/hour.

    In terms of the variables d and c, select an expression that represents the total fuel consumption (in gallons) and the total cost of fuel (in dollars) for the entire journey.

    Make only two selections, one in each column.

	A	B	
	Total Fuel Consumption (gallons)	**Total Cost of Fuel (dollars)**	
A	○	○	$cd/72$
B	○	○	$cd/20$
C	○	○	$c/72d$
D	○	○	$c/20d$
E	○	○	$20cd$

Solve yourself:

2. Given that n people can sit in r chairs arranged in a row in 56 ways; find the possible values of n and r that are consistent with the information provided.

Make one selection in each column.

	A	B	
	n	r	
A	○	○	2
B	○	○	3
C	○	○	4
D	○	○	5
E	○	○	6
F	○	○	8

Solve yourself:

3. Alex can beat Betty in an 800-yard race by 120 yards, Betty can beat Cherry in a 1700-yard race by 200 yards, and Cherry can beat Dirk in a 1200-yard race by 80 yards.

Select the values in yards for "Alex beats Cherry" and "Betty beats Dirk" in a 400-yard race that are consistent with the information provided.

Make only two selections, one in each column.

	A	B	
	Alex beats Cherry	Betty beats Dirk	
A	◯	◯	30
B	◯	◯	50
C	◯	◯	70
D	◯	◯	90
E	◯	◯	100

Solve yourself:

4. Mike, Garry, and Jack are given an assignment to collectively solve a tricky questios. If the probabilities of Mike, Garry, and Jack solving similar questions individually are 1/3, 1/4, and 1/5, respectively, then select the probabilities that the question will be solved and that it will not be solved.

Make only two selections, one in each column.

	A	B	
	Probability that the question will be solved	Probability that the question will not be solved	
A	○	○	1/60
B	○	○	1/12
C	○	○	11/12
D	○	○	2/5
E	○	○	3/5
F	○	○	59/60

Solve yourself:

5. The Midtown City Centre wishes to organize two plays: a Broadway and a Musical. It wants to invite five foreign artists for each play. Four foreign artists for each play have already been finalized.

The center has laid down few conditions for selecting the fifth foreign artist for each play. The conditions are:

(A) No more than one musician should be in any play

(B) A minimum of two theatre artists must be in any play

(C) A maximum of two artists of the same country can be in any play

Broadway Play	Musical
Alicia *(Cinema artist, Kid, U.S.)*	Diego *(Theatre artist, Singer, Argentina)*
Joe *(Cinema artist, Adolescent, UK)*	Pesky *(Cinema artist, Senior, Argentina)*
Xiang *(Cinema artist, Teenager, China)*	Lue *(Theatre artist, Teenager, China)*
Nobita *(Theatre artist, Musician, Japan)*	Leon *(Cinema artist, Kid, U.S.)*

Select which foreign artist given in the table is not eligible to participate in any play, and is eligible to participate in both the plays per the information provided.

Make only two selections, one in each column.

	A	B	
	No Play	**Both Plays**	
A	○	○	Podolsky *(Theatre artist, Musician, U.S.)*
B	○	○	Parker *(Cinema artist, Adolescent, U.K.)*
C	○	○	Li Mao *(Cinema artist, Teenager, China)*
D	○	○	Balki *(Theatre artist, Musician, Argentina)*
E	○	○	Willis *(Theatre artist, Kid, New Zealand)*

Solve yourself:

Practice Questions (Verbal)

6. Scientists at Indiana University in the U.S. claim to have pinpointed a molecule in the bloodstream that identifies people's intent on taking their own lives. These scientists claim that raised levels of this biomarker can predict and thereby prevent suicide attempts. Which of the following information, if true, would best support the argument, and which would best *not* support the argument?

   Make only two selections, one in each column.

	A	B	
	Support	Not Support	
A	○	○	Although medical science has made great strides in identifying biological predictors, claims of predicting exclusively human attributes, such as ethics, love, and free will, and like are overstated.
B	○	○	There are cultural factors. In Japan, for example, suicide can be recognized as noble. In China, unlike in most other countries, more women kill themselves than do men.
C	○	○	The discovery of a blood test that can determine the propensity of a person to commit suicide needs to be hailed as a significant medical breakthrough.
D	○	○	Unlike with the diagnostic tests, the biggest challenge with psychiatry is that those experiencing depression often suppress their suicidal thoughts, making it extremely difficult to gauge the mental health of a patient through traditional psychiatric practices.
E	○	○	In a country where psychiatric problems are perceived as taboo, such diagnostic tests will help people see emotional disorders as treatable medical conditions.

Solve yourself:

7. Two similar farms were planted with the same number of groundnut plants. Organic fertilizer was added only to the first farm's fields. While the first farm harvested 150 tons of groundnuts, the second farm harvested 100 tons. Since nothing else except water was added to both the farms' fields, the first farm's greater yield must have been due to the organic fertilizer.

Select "Strengthen" for the statement that would, if true, most strengthen the argument, and select "Weaken" for the statement that would, if true, most weaken the argument.

Make only two selections, one in each column.

	A	B	
	Strengthen	Weaken	
A	○	○	Another similar farm added synthetic fertilizer and harvested 220 tons of groundnuts.
B	○	○	The size of the nuts harvested from the second farm is no smaller than that of the nuts from the first farm.
C	○	○	The two similar farms differed only with respect to soil composition and basicity, in favor of the first farm.
D	○	○	Many weeds that compete with groundnut plants could not subsist due to the green fertilizer used on the first farm.
E	○	○	Some useful weeds (e.g., Chicory) grown in the second farmhouse drew a good price in the market.

Solve yourself:

7.4 Multi-Source Reasoning

Information for Questions 1–3

Tab 1

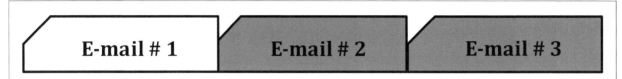

Indian Consultant to Director:

Our team has concluded the analysis of market conditions in India for TopGMAT Inc. The company's 10 existing franchises continue to perform very well. Given recent performance and market trends, we project that these franchises will continue to perform well in the conceivable future. Furthermore, our analysis recommends that scheduled openings of five additional Indian franchises should be fruitful. However, our research further suggests that those five additional franchises will fully saturate the Indian market with your unique brand of the GMAT test preparation course.

Tab 2

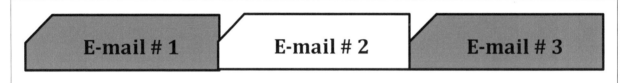

Director to Employees:

The company is exceedingly proud of our state-of-the-art GMAT test preparation course. In less than five years, we have gone from one small franchise in Mumbai to over 10 franchises across India. We must hate the word "stagnancy." Over the next few months, the president and I will be aggressively planning the next phase of our growth. We are considering all options and, as always, welcome any input you may have.

Tab 3

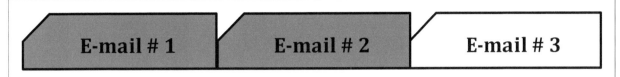

Franchising Advisor to President:

I thank you and TopGMAT Inc. for allowing us to serve you. Over the past five years, our company has provided sound franchising guidance to over 50 companies in the US. We look forward to working with you in the years ahead. You have done tremendously well so far with your 10 Indian franchises. However, we understand your need to expand beyond India. Franchising is an excellent method of expanding rapidly. By franchising, you can grow on the investment of entrepreneurs across the country. These entrepreneurs provide vital knowledge of their home market, while you provide in-depth knowledge of TopGMAT's innovative curriculum and matchless branding.

Questions 1–3

1. What does the Director mean when he says, "We must hate the word stagnancy"?

   (A) An aggressive plan to open more TopGMAT test-prep franchises in India.

   (B) An aggressive plan to open more TopGMAT test-prep franchises in other countries, including India.

   (C) An aggressive plan to offer other courses apart from GMAT courses in other countries, including India.

   (D) An aggressive plan to expand business in general—nothing specific.

   (E) An aggressive plan to venture into school and college business.

   Solve yourself:

2. Consider each of the following statements. Does the information in the three e-mails support the following inferences?

	Yes	No	
A	○	○	The Indian consultant believes that the franchise option will work better if TopGMAT Inc. leverages on the crucial knowledge that entrepreneurs have about their home market.
B	○	○	The Indian consultant is less optimistic about opening more than 15 franchises in India.
C	○	○	If TopGMAT Inc. expands by franchising in other countries, it is certain to succeed.

   Solve yourself:

3. Consider each of the following statements. Does the information in the three e-mails support the following inferences?

	Yes	No	
A	○	○	The Indian market can accommodate only 10 TopGMAT franchise centers.
B	○	○	The Director has decided that franchising is the next phase of expansion.
C	○	○	Expansion beyond India is important to the future of TopGMAT Inc.

Solve yourself:

Information for Questions 4–6

Tab 1

Incentive | Sales

A super-mall, S-Mart, wants to promote the availability of value-for-money food. To promote caterers, S-Mart does not charge commission to the vendors; instead it offers incentives.

The S-Mart Incentive Program

Regular pizzas sold per week	Incentive (dollars)
100 or more	10
200 or more	20
300 or more	50
500 or more	100

Tab 2

Incentive | Sales

Ben is a small time caterer who sells fresh pizzas at S-Mart. Ben spent $1750 to set up the kitchen and spends $20 per week on operating expenses.

Pizza Prices and Units Sold by Ben

Pizza	Price per piece (dollars)	Average number of units sold per week
Regular Pizza	3	40
Premium Topping	0.75	10
Popular Topping	0.50	15

Questions 4–6

4. What would be the difference between the maximum and the minimum sales for Ben if he sold 700 regular pizzas in four weeks?

   (A) $40

   (B) $50

   (C) $60

   (D) $70

   (E) $80

   Solve yourself:

5. If Ben sells 150 regular pizzas, 10 premium toppings, and 5 popular toppings per week, from which week onwards, he will start making a profit?

   (A) Third

   (B) Fourth

   (C) Fifth

   (D) Sixth

   (E) Seventh

   Solve yourself:

6. For each of the following statements, select "Earn more," if the following scenario makes Ben earn more compared to the current sales and pricing structure as given in tab 2; otherwise select "Earn less."

	Earn more	Earn less	
A	○	○	Ben decreases the price of regular pizza to $1.15 and leaves the prices of toppings the same. His regular pizza sales increase to 100/week but toppings sales remain the same.
B	○	○	Ben decreases the price of regular pizza to $1.00 and increases the prices of each topping by $0.25. His regular pizza sales increase to 120/week; his premium topping sales remain the same but popular topping sales become zero.
C	○	○	Ben increases the price of regular pizza to $6 and increases the prices of each topping by $0.25. His regular pizza sales decrease to 20/week, premium topping sales decrease to 5 and popular topping sales decrease to 10.

Solve yourself:

Chapter 8

Answer Key

Table Analysis

Q1	Q2	Q3	Q4
No, Yes, Yes	No, No, No	Yes, No, Yes	Yes, Yes, No

Graphics Interpretation

Q1	Q2	Q3	Q4	Q5
B, D	A, C	D, D	A, A	B, B

2-Part Analysis

Q1	Q2	Q3	Q4	Q5	Q6	Q7
A, B	A, F	E, C	E, D	C, E	D, A	D, C

Multi-Source Reasoning

Q1	Q2	Q3	Q4	Q5	Q6
D	No, Yes, No	No, No, Yes	E	B	More, More, Less

Chapter 9

Solutions

9.1   Table Analysis

1. **Solution—Part A**

What does "consistency" mean? It means the data values are relatively close to each other. You can measure the consistency using many parameters, such as range of data, standard deviation, mean deviation, and others. The question asks you to measure the consistency using the parameter, Range. Note that:

$$\text{Range} = \text{Highest value in a dataset} - \text{Lowest value in a dataset}$$

To approach this question, you can sort the table either by column 2 (Grade), or by column 5 (IQ). We prefer sorting by column 2 (Grade). Have a look at the image given below.

Sorted by column 2

Col 1	Col 2	Col 3	Col 4	Col 5		
Months	**Grade**	**Average maximum Score**	**Average minimum Score**	**Intelligence Quotient**		
August	X	66	58	116		
December	X	71	52	117		
July	X	71	55	115		Range (X) = 121 − 115 = 6
November	X	81	62	119		
October	X	68	54	121		
September	X	72	52	121		
August	XII	68	55	120		
December	XII	70	49	114		Range (XII) = 120 − 114 = 6
July	XII	72	45	116		
November	XII	69	51	118		
October	XII	69	45	120		
September	XII	75	56	114		

It is clear from the sorted table that the range for both the grades are equal (Range = 6). The correct answer to part A is "No".

Solution—Part B

"Deviation" means the difference between two values. Here, the question wants you to compare the greatest deviations between the average maximum score and the average minimum score for both the grades—X and XII. Here,

$$\text{Deviation} = \text{Average maximum score} - \text{Average minimum score}$$

It is not advisable to calculate the deviations for all the 12 data points. An efficient approach is to quickly scan through columns 4 and 5 and observe which of the differences could be the highest. The deviation $72 - 45 = 27$ for the month of July for grade XII may be the highest. The closest to this for grade X seems to be the deviation $72 - 52 = 20$ for the month of September, but it is smaller.

The correct answer to part B is "Yes".

Solution—Part C

The mean average minimum score for August is for grades X and XII: $(58 + 55)/2 = 56.5$. Similarly, the mean average minimum score for July is $(45 + 55)/2 = 50$, and that for December is $(52 + 49)/2 = 50.5$.

Since 56.5 is greater than both 50 and 50.5, the statement is correct. Remember that had the mean average minimum score for August been greater than that for either of the other two months, and lesser than that for the other month, the answer would have been "No".

The correct answer to part C is "Yes".

2. Solution—Part A

The question wants you to find out whether or not the mean score for Math is greater than its median score.

Calculating median is a comparatively easy task than calculating the mean as mean may involve calculation. Hence, you should calculate the median first.

$$\text{Median of Math scores} = \text{Value of the } \left(\frac{n+1}{2}\right)^{th} \text{ student's score,}$$

where n is number of students

To get the values, sort the table by column 2 (Math). See the sorted table given below. Note that if $\frac{n+1}{2}$ is a fraction, take the average of the two values at the integer indices on either side of the result.

Sorted by column 2

Col 1	Col 2	Col 3	Col 4	Col 5
Students	**Math (100**	**Craft (25)**	**English (50)**	**Science (100)**
Sean	8	22	50	47
Marrie	10	20	6	45
Justin	12	18	5	35
Matt	54	22	45	39
Garysson	59			33
Joe	64	Median of Math		31
Jack	69	= (64+69)/2 = 66.5		27
Elad	74	5	49	84
Lucy	79	7	33	29
Angelo	84	9	35	35
Kevin	89	20	39	37
Mehul	94	13	43	41

According to the chart, the median score for Math is 66.5.

Now, calculate the mean score for Math.

To calculate the mean, you might think that you have to sum all the 12 scores and divide the sum by 12. Despite having the luxury of an online calculator, this is a time-consuming process. The GMAT never asks a question that consumes a disproportionately high amount of time. So, there must be an alternate approach.

Observe that the last nine cells in column 2 have scores ranging from 54 to 94, in a sequence with an interval of 5. The middle-most value is 74. You can use this to quickly calculate the sum of all the scores: $(8 + 10 + 12) + 74 \times 9 = 696$.

You *should* use the online calculator for this. The mean score: $696/12 = 58$.

It is clear that the mean score, 58, is less than its median score of 66.5.

The correct answer to part A is "No".

Solution—Part B

A question asks whether it would affect the median scores for Math and for Science, if Math and Science scores for Justine were swapped.

Currently, Justine's Math and Science scores are 12 and 35, respectively. After swapping them, they would become 35 and 12, respectively.

You have already calculated the median score for Math in Part A of the question: 66.5. Since the wrong value (35) and the correct value (12) are less than the median value (66.5), the median score for Math would not be impacted. More precisely, when the column 2 values are arranged in ascending order, both 12 and 35 would appear before the median value of 66.5, irrespective of whether they are: 12 and 35 or 35 and 12.

Now, calculate the median score for Science.

First, sort the table by column 5 (Science), given below.

Sorted by column 5

	Col 1	Col 2	Col 3	Col 4	Col 5
	Students	Math (100)	Craft (25)	English (50)	Science (100)
Jack	69	7	41	27
Lucy	79			29
Joe	64			31
Garysson	59			33
Justin	**12**	18	5	**35**
Angelo	84			**35**
Kevin	89	Median of Science = (35+37)/2 = 36		**37**
Matt	54			39
Mehul	94	13	43	41
Marrie	10	20	6	45
Sean	8	22	50	47
Elad	74	5	49	84

You can see in the chart that the median score for Science is 36. Again, both the wrong and the correct values (12 and 35) are less than the median value 36. With the same reasoning as used above, the median score for Science would not be impacted.

The correct answer to part B is "No".

What if the median score for Math was impacted but that for Science was not? In that case, the answer still would have been "No". You will seldom find this kind of ambiguous question in GMAT.

What if the same mixup had occurred with Jack's scores instead of Justine's?

Jack's scores for Math and Science are 69 and 27, respectively. Well, in that case, the median scores for Math as well as for Science would have been impacted.

Solution—Part C

The question asks whether the median score for Science would increase by 2 points over its current value, if scores of two new students, Suzi and McDonald, were included in the table. Their scores for Science are 10 and 45, respectively.

You know that median is the middle-most element(s) of a set of elements sorted in ascending/descending order. Adding one element above and one below the median does not change the middle-most element(s) of the list. Since you know the median score for Science is 36, so by adding 10 (less than 36) and 45 (greater than 36) would not change the median.

The correct answer to part C is "No".

What if the Science scores for Suzi and McDonald were 40 and 45 respectively? Well, in that case, the median score for science would have certainly increased by 2 points.

3. Solution—Part A

Sorted by column 5

Col 4	Col 5
Minimum sales per month	**Manager's comments on sales**
3	Average
1	Average
5	Average
6	Average
2	Average
6	Average
11	**Average**
4	Below average
8	**High**
11	High
11	High
13	High
12	High
10	**High**
15	High
10	**High**
16	High
12	High
16	High
18	High
20	High
19	High
0	Low
2	Low

The question asks whether there are two or more "High-sales" cars (Manager's criterion) whose minimum sales per month are less than the highest minimum sales per month of a car reported either "Average-sales", "Below-average-sales", or "Low-sales".

The best approach to sort the table by column 5 (Managers's comments on sales).

Scan through column 4 (Minimum sales per month) in the chart and pinpoint the highest values for cars that reported "Average-sales", "Below-average-sales", or "Low-sales". There are eight qualifying cells (seven "Average-sales"; one "Below-average-sales") lying on the top and two cells (two "Low-sales") lying at the bottom. The highest value among these 10 cells is 11.

Again, quickly run through the column 4 and find the values less than 11 for the cars that reported "High sales". These values are 8, 10, and 10. So, three (at least two) cars reporting "High sales" had minimum sales per month lower than the highest minimum sales per month of cars which did not have "High sales".

The correct answer to part A is "Yes".

Solution—Part B

Sorted by column 3

Col 3	Col 4
Maximum sales per month	**Minimum sales per month**
6	0
7	2
8	4
9	3
10	1
10	5
10	6
11	2
11	6
16	8
19	11
20	11
20	13
21	11
21	12
21	10
21	15
21	10
22	16
22	12
23	16
25	18
26	20
27	19

This is a question on the concept of "correlation". Hopefully, you have already familiarized yourself with the concept of correlation discussed in this book. Here's a recap:

Two entities are positively correlated if both of them either increase or decrease in tandem. Two entities are negatively correlated if one entity decreases in value when the other increases in value. The two entities are not correlated if the increase or the decrease in the value of one entity cannot be related to the increase or the decrease in the value of the other.

Sort the table by column 3 (Maximum sales per month). The values will be arranged in ascending order or, in other words, in an increasing trend.

Now observe how the other entity in column 4 (Minimum sales per month) behaves. In the chart, the downward arrows mark runs of values that are increasing, while the arrows going up do so for values that are decreasing. As there are enough upward arrows and enough downward arrows, so, for these two entities, you cannot conclude that they are perfectly correlated. You need to analyze further.

Notice that the downward arrows are longer in length than are upward arrows. This means that most values in column 4 are increasing with the increases in column 3's values, implying that they have—though not perfect—a strong positive correlation.

The correct answer to part B is "No".

Solution—Part C

Sorted by column 2

Col 2	Col 3
Company	**Maximum sales per month**
BMW	6
BMW	8
BMW	9
BMW	10
BMW	11
BMW	22
Ford Motors	7
Ford Motors	10
Ford Motors	21
General Motors	10
General Motors	21
General Motors	22
Hyundai	20
Hyundai	21
Hyundai	21
Hyundai	27
Nissan	11
Nissan	16
Nissan	19
Nissan	20
Nissan	21
Nissan	23
Nissan	25
Nissan	26

The question wants you to find out if the mean maximum sales per month for Hyundai cars is greater than the mean maximum sales per month for BMW cars.

Sort the table by column 2 (Company).

In the chart, there are six BMW cars and four Hyundai cars.

Observe that the highest value for Hyundai cars (27) is greater than that for BMW cars (22), and that all other values for Hyundai cars are greater than those for BMW cars. Hence, without calculation, you can conclude that the mean maximum sales per month for Hyundai cars is greater than that for BMW cars.

The correct answer to part C is "Yes".

4. Solution—Part A

The question wants you to find out whether the average scores per match for Sachin's teams are more than those for other teams (Teams that do not include Sachin).

To get the answer, sort the table by column 6 (Average score per match). This will make sure that matches with higher average scores group in the bottom cells.

Sorted by column 6

Col 4	Col 5	Col 6
Most Valuable Player	**Number of matches played**	**Average score per match**
Mahela	22	121
Gayle	74	121
Kumara	24	124
Clarke	74	125
Kumara	77	128
Dhoni, Nannes	85	144
Clarke, Kumara	14	144
Mahela, Sehwag	81	145
Gambhir, Nannes	11	152
Malinga, Gayle	15	153
Clarke, Gayle	21	154
Gambhir	80	154
Sachin, Mahela	12	**154**
Sachin	26	**155**
Sachin, Malinga	83	**165**

Note that in column 4, the last three cells are occupied by Sachin, implying that each team in which Sachin plays scored higher average score.

The correct answer for part A is "Yes".

Solution—Part B

The question wants you to find out whether it is likely that the teams that included Clarke did not win a tournament.

Sorted by column 3

Col 3	Col 4	Col 5	Col 6	Col 7
Country	Most Valuable Player	Number of matches played	Average score per match	% of matches won
Australia	Mahela	22	121	87
Australia	Kumara	24	124	83
Australia	**Clarke**, Gayle	21	154	**43**
Australia	Sachin	26	155	46
India	Gayle	74	121	45
India	**Clarke**	74	125	**42**
India	Kumara	77	128	46
India	Dhoni, Nannes	85	144	46
India	Mahela, Sehwag	81	145	54
India	Gambhir	80	154	81
India	Sachin, Malinga	83	165	83
Sri Lanka	**Clarke**, Kumara	14	144	**43**
Sri Lanka	Gambhir, Nannes	11	152	43
Sri Lanka	Malinga, Gayle	15	153	47
Sri Lanka	Sachin, Mahela	12	154	91

In the chart, you would observe that column 7 (% of matches won) indicates that none of Clarke's teams have won more than 50% of their matches. Since the result of any match is a win/loss (less than 50% win implies more loss), it is likely that no team that included Clarke would have won the tournament.

The correct answer for part B is "Yes".

Solution—Part C

The question wants you to find out whether the mean average score for the Australian teams is more than the mean average score for the Sri Lankan teams.

To get this, sort the table by column 3 (Country). This will group rows of Australia and Sri Lanka. Refer to the image given in Solution—Part B of the question. To actually calculate the mean for each team, you would have to use eight data; however here is no need for this, mere observation is sufficient. This question does not want a numerical answer. It simply wants you to compare two values in terms of more or less.

Refer column 6, Sri Lankan teams have scored between 150-155 three times, and more than 140 once, while Australian teams have scored 150-155 only two times, and the other two scores being less than 125. You can thus deduce that the mean for Sri Lankan teams would be more than that for Australian teams.

The correct answer for part C is "No".

9.2   Graphics Interpretation

1.   Solution—Part A

You have to calculate:

$$\frac{\text{Total revenue from taxi in yr. 2006}}{\text{Total revenue from bus in yr. 2006}}$$

$$\frac{\text{Total revenue from taxi in yr. 2006}}{\text{Total revenue from bus in yr. 2006}} = \frac{\text{\# of taxi commuters} \times \text{Taxi fare/passenger}}{\text{\# of bus commuters} \times \text{Bus fare/passenger}}$$

$$\Rightarrow \frac{\approx 160\text{M} \times 30}{\approx 320\text{M} \times 0.75} \cong 20:1$$

The correct answer for part A is option B.

Solution—Part B

You have to find out what the number of taxi passengers in the year 2010 would be if the growth rate in the number of such passengers during 2009-2010 was the same as from 2008-2009. You have to calculate:

$$\text{Number of passengers}\big|_{2010} = \text{Number of passengers}\big|_{2009} \times \left(1 + \text{Growth rate}\big|_{2008\text{-}2009}\right)$$

First calculate:

$$\text{Growth rate}\big|_{2008\text{-}2009} = \frac{(\text{Taxi commuters in 2009} - \text{Taxi commuters in 2008})}{\text{Taxi commuters in 2008}} \times 100\%$$

$$= \frac{\approx 225M - \approx 175M}{\approx 175\text{M}} \times 100\%$$

$$\cong \frac{200}{7}\%$$

So,

$$\text{Number of passengers}\big|_{2010} \cong 225\text{M} \times \left(1 + \frac{200}{7}\%\right) \cong 225\text{M} \times \left(1 + \frac{2}{7}\right) \cong 289.3\text{M}.$$

Do use the calculator.

The correct answer for part B is option D.

2. **Solution—Part A**

You have to calculate:

Number of Engineering undergrads – Number of Management undergrads

In the pie chart, you will find that the percentage of Engineering undergrads and Management undergrads are 18% and 12%, respectively. So,

Number of Engineering – Number of Management undergrads = 18% – 12% = 6%

Had you known the value of total number of undergrads, you can get the answer. However, you don't really need to know it.

You already know that the number of the Art undergrads equals 6% of the total student population, and since this is the number you're looking for, you don't need to calculate it. Simply make use of number of Art undergrads, which is 126.

The correct answer to part A is option A.

Solution—Part B

After answering Part A, you might be tempted to simply calculate:

Number of Engineering – Number of Science undergrads = 18% – 12% = 6%,

as the answer, however 6% is wrong. What you really need to calculate is:

$$\frac{\text{Number of Engineering undergrads – Number of Science undergrads}}{\text{Number of Science undergrads}} \times 100\%$$

$$= \frac{18\% \text{ of total undergrads} - 12\% \text{ of total undergrads}}{12\% \text{ of total undergrads}} \times 100\%$$

$$= \left(\frac{18\% - 12\%}{12\%}\right) \times 100\% = 50\%$$

You need not know the value of total number of undergrads, as it cancels out.

Notice that the denominator is the number of Science undergrads (12% of total undergrads) and not the number of Engineering undergrads (18% of total undergrads). Had you mistakenly put the number of Engineering undergrads in the denominator, you would have wrongly answered the questions as 33.33%.

The correct answer to part B is option C.

3. Solution—Part A

The question is pretty simple. It is a multiple-column chart presenting the percent distribution of household owners of seven electronic gadgets, for the years 2009 and 2012.

Look at the first part of the question.

> During the three-year period, the maximum percentage increase in the popularity registered by an electronic goods equals _____ %. (Assume that the population of household owners was same for both the years).

The question wants you to find out two things:

(1) The goods that had the maximum percent growth from the year 2009 to 2012, and

(2) The percent growth for that goods during the period

Start with the first part.

The percent growth is calculated by:

$$\frac{\text{Growth}}{\text{Base value}} \times 100\% = \frac{\text{Value in 2012} - \text{Value in 2009}}{\text{Value in 2009}} \times 100\%$$

Since the population of household owners was same in both the years, you can ignore its effect.

Looking at the chart, you can infer that fridges, smartphones, and cameras had good absolute growth in the years 2009 to 2012. So, the goods with maximum percent-growth would be one among these.

Now, which goods among the three would be the answer? Would it be the one which had maximum absolute growth in the years 2009 to 2012? The answer is, "No, not necessarily." The goods would be the one for which the ratio of

$$\frac{\text{Growth}}{\text{Value in 2009}} \text{ is the highest.}$$

To deduce that, the numerator (Growth) should be maximized and the denominator (Value in 2009) should be minimized.

It is obvious that the answer would be Camera.

So, what is the value of percent growth for Camera?

We know that:

$$\text{Percent growth} = \frac{\text{Value in 2012} - \text{Value in 2009}}{\text{Value in 2009}} \times 100\% = \frac{\approx 62 - 40}{40} \times 100\% = \frac{\approx 22}{40} \times 100\% \cong 55\%.$$

The closest answer is option D.

Though the absolute growth for Fridge is also $\cong 22$, its Percent growth is comparatively less.

$$\text{Percent growth} = \frac{\approx 95 - 72}{72} \times 100\% = \frac{\approx 23}{72} \times 100\% \cong 32\%.$$

Solution—Part B

Look at the second part of the question.

> If the number of owners increased from 606 million in the year 2009 to 1210 million in the year 2012, then the number of new fridges purchased between 2009 and 2012 is _____ million. (Assume that no household owner has sold/discarded a fridge during the period.)

Calculate:

$$\text{\# of new fridges} = (\% \text{ owners'}12 \times \text{population'}12) - (\% \text{ owners'}09 \times \text{population'}09)$$

$$= (95\% \times 1210) - (72\% \times 606) \cong 713\text{M. (Use calculator)}$$

The closest answer is option D.

4. **Solution—Part A**

To find the value of Rupee 5500 in Dinar, first you need to convert Rupees 5500 to Dollar and then Dollar to Dinar since the Rupees-to-Dinar conversion is not given in the graph.

Beware that the secondary-axis is calibrated using solid grey lines, and the primary axis is calibrated using dashed black lines.

From the graph, the Rupees-to-Dollar rate as on July 1 is $\approx$ 57. So, Rupees 5500 would equal 5500/57 = \$96.49. Again, Dollars-to-Dinar rate on July 1 is 3.5. Beware! You must read the values from the secondary axis. Hence, Rupees 5500 or \$96.49 = 96.49/3.5 = Dinar 27.57. The closest answer in the options is Dinar 27.81.

The correct answer to part A is option A.

Solution—Part B

The person can buy the Mac if he has the money in a particular currency greater than or equal to the cost of the Mac (Real 2400). Let us calculate the cost of the Mac in different currencies.

On Sept 1, the Real-to-Dollar rate is 2.4. So, the cost of Mac in equivalent Dollars for Real 2400 equals:

$$2400/2.4 = \$1000.$$

The man has \$1100 (more than \$1000), so he can buy the Mac spending only Dollars.

Similarly, the Rupees-to-Dollar rate is $\approx$ 62. So, the cost of Mac in equivalent Rupees equals

$$\$1000 = \text{Rupees } (1000 \times 62) = \text{Rupees } 62,000.$$

The man has only Rupees 50,000 (less than Rupees 62000), so he cannot buy the Mac spending only Rupees.

Similarly, the Dollar-to-Dinar rate is $\approx$ 3.4. So, the equivalent Dinar equals

$$\$1000 = (1000/3.4) \text{ Dinar} = 277.8 \text{ Dinar}.$$

The man has only Dinar 250 (less than Dinar 277.8), so he cannot buy the Mac spending only Dinar.

Hence, he can buy the Mac only using Dollars.

The correct answer to part B is option A.

5. **Solution—Part A**

From the second 100% stacked bar, you find that 25% of the Humanities students play Tennis. From the first 100% stacked bar, you find that 60% of the students are belong to Humanities majors.

This means that of the total students in the school, 25% of 60% = 15% play Tennis.

The correct answer is option B.

Solution—Part B

From the chart, you can see that 50% Humanities students who play soccer are Mexican. Hence, you can deduce that the total number of soccer playing Humanities students is: $\dfrac{80}{50\%}$ = 160. These 160 students are in fact 40% of the Humanities students. (Read the data from the second bar.) Hence, you can deduce that the total number of Humanities students is: $\dfrac{160}{40\%}$ = 400.

Again, from the first bar, you can see that 60% of the students in the school are Humanities students.

Hence, you can deduce that the total number of Management students is

$$400 \times \left(\frac{15\%}{60\%}\right) = 100.$$

The correct answer to part B is option B.

9.3   2-Part Analysis

Practice Questions (Quants)

1. **Solution—Both Parts**

   Understand the question. It is pretty simple. You have to find out the total fuel consumption (gallons) and the total cost of fuel (dollars) for the entire journey of d miles. The information given is the average speed (72 miles/hour), the fuel consumption per hour (c gallons/hr.), and the cost of fuel ($3.60/gallon).

   You can infer that this is a typical speed-time-distance question, with an addition information about the cost of fuel.

   First, you should always observe the given options, to short-list probable options or eliminate a few non-probable options. However, here there is no option that you can easily eliminate.

   Determine the total fuel consumption. You can calculate the total fuel consumption (in gallons) by multiplying the average fuel consumed per hour with the total hours of travel.

   Total fuel consumption (gallons) = (Average fuel consumed/hour) × (Total hours of travel)
   $$= c \times (d/72) = cd/72 \text{ gallons}$$

   So, option A is the answer for the first part.

   You calculate the total cost of fuel by:

   Total cost of fuel (dollars) = Total fuel consumption (gallons) × Cost of fuel
   $$= (cd/72) \times 3.60 = \$cd/20$$

   So, option B is the answer for the second part.

   The correct answers are options A and B.

2. **Solution—Both Parts**

   This is a question on arrangement; hence, you must apply permutation instead of combination. Note that the number of people, n, must be less than or equal to the number of chairs, r.

   Given that $P_n^r = 56$. Note that it is *not* $P_r^n = 56$.

   By hit and trial, we can deduce that $P_n^r = 56 = 8.7 = P_2^8$. The correct answers are $n = 2$ and $r = 8$. Beware that answering $n = 8$ and $r = 2$ would be wrong.

   Finally, note that you must not solve this problem using combination, in which you would use $C_n^r = 56$. This gives $r = 8$ and $n = 3$, which are the wrong values.

   The correct answers are options A and F.

3. **Solution—Both Parts**

   This is a question answered by applying the concept of continued proportion. You can get the proportion of Alex : Betty : Cherry : Dirk by making a table such as following:

	Alex	Betty	Cherry	Dirk
		800	800 − 120 = 680		
			1700	1700 − 200 = 1500	
				1200	1200 − 80 = 1120
Continued Proportion	800	680	$\frac{1500}{1700} \times 680 = 600$	$\frac{1120}{1200} \times 600 = 560$

   So, Alex : Betty : Cherry : Dirk :: 800 : 680 : 600 : 560.

   This means that Alex will beat Cherry by 800 − 600 = 200 yards in an 800-yard race. In other words, Alex can beat Cherry by 100 yards in a 400-yard race.

   Similarly, Betty can beat Dirk by 680 − 560 = 120 yards in a 680-yard race. In other words, Betty will beat Dirk by $\left[\dfrac{120}{680}\right] \times 400 = 70$ yards in a 400-yard race.

   The correct answers are options E and C.

   Make sure that you mark the answers correctly. Marking options C and E would be wrong.

4. **Solution—Both Parts**

You know that:

Probability that an event will occur + Probability that an event will not occur = 1.

You can write it as $p + q = 1$, where

$$p = \text{Probability of an even to occur}$$

and

$$q = \text{Probability of an even not to occur}$$

You should first calculate q, because the questions will not be solved under only one condition: when each of Mike, Garry, and Jack are not able to solve the questions. Therefore,

Probability of not solving the questions

= Product of the probabilities that Mike could not solve,

Garry could not solve, and Jack could not solve

$$= \left(1 - \tfrac{1}{3}\right)\left(1 - \tfrac{1}{4}\right)\left(1 - \tfrac{1}{5}\right) = \tfrac{2}{3} \times \tfrac{3}{4} \times \tfrac{4}{5} = \tfrac{2}{5}$$

The correct answer for second part of the question is option D. Hence,

⇒ Probability of solving the questions = 1 − Probability of not solving the questions

$$= 1 - \tfrac{2}{5} = \tfrac{3}{5}.$$

The correct answer for first part of the question is option E.

The correct answers are options E and D.

5. Solution—Both Parts

The question is pretty simple. You are given certain constraints on selecting the fifth artist for each play.

The conditions are:

(A) Musicians ≤ 1

(B) Theatre artists ≥ 2

(C) Same nationality artists ≤ 2

Let us disciss each option one by one.

(A) Parker *(Cinema artist, Adolescent, UK)* cannot be selected for the first play, as he is not a theatre artist. There must be at least two theatre artists in each play. He can, however, be selected for the second play.

(B) Li Mao *(Cinema artist, Teenager, China)* cannot be selected for the first play, as he is not a theatre artist. There must be at least two theatre artists in each play. He can, however, be selected for the second play.

(C) Balki *(Theatre artist, Musician, Argentina)* cannot be selected for any play. He cannot be selected for the first play, as he is a musician. There must not be two musicians in any play. He also cannot be selected for the second play, as he is an Argentinean. There must not be more than two Argentineans in any play. This is the correct answer for Part A.

(D) Podolsky *(Theatre artist, Musician, U.S.)* cannot be selected for the first play, as he is a musician. There must not be two musicians in any play. He can, however, be selected for the second play.

(E) Willis *(Theatre artist, Kid, New Zealand)* can be selected for both the plays. This is the correct answer for Part B.

The correct answers are options C and E.

Practice Questions (Verbal)

6. *Claim*: A diagnostic test measuring the levels of biomarker (a molecule in the blood-stream) can predict and prevent suicide attempts.

Answer Choice Explanation

(A) This is the correct answer for the second part of the question. It clearly goes against the argument. It raises doubt over the test's capability to measure such humanist attributes as ethics, love, free will, and like. It can be inferred that biological predictors will not be able to measure emotions, such as suicidal tendencies.

(B) Cultural factors are out of scope. It neither supports nor weakens the claim.

(C) How the discovery of this blood test should be viewed is irrelevant. There is no logical reason to believe that it is pertinent to the claim. It neither supports nor weakens the claim.

(D) This is the correct answer for the first part of the question. It argues that traditional psychiatry falters at detecting suicidal tendencies, implying that this diagnostic test would help gauge a subject's mental health.

(E) This option talks about emotional disorders in general and is not focused on suicides. It neither supports nor weakens the claim.

Between options D and E, D is the best choice of one that supports the argument.

The correct answers are options D and A.

7. *Conclusion:* The larger harvest from the first farm must have been caused by the organic fertilizer.

Predicting a Strengthener and a Weakener

Predictive Strengthener: A similar farm that treated its crop with organic fertilizer harvested nearly 150 tons.

Predictive Weakener 1: There is a factor which aids in increasing groundnut harvest on the first farm.

Predictive Weakener 2: There is a factor which impedes groundnut harvest on the second farm.

Answer Choice Explanation

(A) The effects of synthetic fertilizers are outside the scope of the argument.

(B) The size of nuts is outside the scope of the argument. The argument is concerned only about the size of harvests.

(C) This option is a weakener. Better soil properties may have aided the first farm's harvest. This option weakens the conclusion. This is the answer of the second part.

(D) This option is a strengthener. It explains why organic fertilizer is effective against weeds, and thus helped the harvest. It strengthens the conclusion. This is the answer of the first part.

(E) Weed harvest and its commercial value are outside the scope of the argument.

The correct answers are options D and C.

9.4 Multi-Source Reasoning

Questions 1–3

1. Refer to the last sentence in Tab 2, where the director states, "*We are considering all our options and, as always, welcome any input you may have.*" His intent is to expand the business. There is no specific plan laid down so far. He will come up with one once he discusses with the president.

   The correct answer is option D.

2. *Part A:*
   No, that is the opinion of the Franchise Advisor.

   The correct answer is "No".

   Part B:
   Yes. He states, "*However, our research further suggests that those five additional franchises will fully saturate the Indian market...*"

   The correct answer is "Yes".

   Part C:
   You cannot infer this. The success of franchises is talked about with reference to the Indian market only.

   The correct answer is "No".

3. *Part A:*
   Both the director and franchising consultant only discuss the existing 10 franchises, but the Indian consultant explicitly states that the Indian market has room for an additional five franchises.

   The correct answer is "No".

   Part B:
   While the franchising advisor assumes that expansion must occur through franchising, the director only states, "*We are considering all of our options...*"

   The correct answer is "No".

   Part C:
   All three stakeholders—the director, the franchise advisor, and the Indian consultant—explicitly express their opinion about growing outside India market.

   The correct answer is "Yes".

Questions 4–6

4. A week-wise distribution of 700 pizzas in four weeks is not given in the question. As for Ben's gross sales, he is going to earn the same despite selling more pizzas in any week(s) and fewer in other week(s).

   However, a week-wise distribution of 700 units would impact his incentives from S-Mart.

   Consider some possible scenarios of Ben selling 700 pizzas in four weeks:

   $$(W1, W2, W3, W4) : (0, 0, 0, 700); (200, 200, 200, 100); (100, 100, 200, 300); (0, 200, 200, 300).$$

   There could be many other scenarios too. Since the maximum incentive by S-Mart is when Ben sells "500 or more" pizza in a week. To maximize his incentives, Ben could sell in the following way:
   $$(W1, W2, W3, W4) : (500, 200, 0, 0)$$

   That would earn him $100 + 20 + 0 + 0 = \$120$, whereas if he had sold the following way:

   $$(W1, W2, W3, W4) : (99, 99, 251, 251)$$

   Ben's incentive would be minimum, and he will earn $0 + 0 + 20 + 20 = \$40$. The difference is $\$120 - \$40 = \$80$.

   The correct answer is option E.

5. Ben will start making a profit starting the week he fully recovers his investment. In other words, when his sales exceed his investment, he will start to make a profit.

   Say, he starts making profit in x^{th} week, then:

   Investment $= 1750 + 20x$

   Sales = Sales from pizzas, premium toppings, and popular toppings, + Incentives

   $$= (150 \times 3 \times x + 10 \times 0.75 \times x + 5 \times 0.50 \times x) + 10 \times x$$

   So, if

   $$(1750 + 20x) < (150 \times 3x + 10 \times 0.75x + 5 \times 0.50x + 10x), \text{ Ben makes profit.}$$

   Solving above, we get $x > 3.88$. Since $x > 3.88$ weeks, Ben will make profit from the fourth week onwards.

   The correct answer is option B.

6. First calculate Ben's current earning. It is $3 \times 40 + 0.75 \times 10 + 0.50 \times 15 = \$135$.

Part A:

Earning in this scenario would be $1.15 \times 100 + 0.75 \times 10 + 0.50 \times 15 = \$130$. If you think the earnings would decrease, you missed the incentive part. Ben is eligible for a \$10 incentive, because he sold 100 pizzas in a week. So his earnings are $130 + 10 = \$140$.

The answer is: Ben earns more (\$140 > \$135).

Part B:

Earning in this scenario would be $[1 \times 120 + (0.75 + 0.25) \times 10 + (0.50 + 0.25) \times 0] + 10 = \$140$. Ben is eligible for a \$10 incentive, because he sold 100 pizzas in a week.

The answer is: Ben earns more (\$140 > \$135).

Part C:

Earning in this scenario would be $6.20 + 1.5 + 0.75 \times 10 = \$132.50$.

The answer is: Ben earns less (\$132.50 < \$135).

Chapter 10

Talk to Us

Email us if you want us to send you an Excel file with 10 tables of Table Analysis questions. We will send you filter-enabled tables so you can practice in a computer-enabled environment.

Email us in the following format:

To: info@manhattanreview.com

Subject: TA tables

Hi,

Please mail me Excel spreadsheets of TA tables.

⟨Your name⟩
⟨Your contact number⟩

Have a Question?

Email your questions to info@manhattanreview.com. We will be happy to answer you. Your questions can be related to a concept, an application of a concept, an explanation of a question, a suggestion for an alternate approach, or anything else you wish to ask regarding the GMAT.

Please mention the page number when quoting from the book.

Best of luck!

Prof. Dr. Joern Meissner
& The Manhattan Review Team

Printed in Poland
by Amazon Fulfillment
Poland Sp. z o.o., Wrocław